God! Do You Hear Me?

M. O. Owens, Jr.

God! Do You Hear Me?
Copyright © 2009 Milum Owens. All rights reserved. No part of this book may be reproduced or retransmitted in any form or by any means without the written permission of the publisher.

Published by Wheatmark®
610 East Delano Street, Suite 104, Tucson, Arizona 85705 U.S.A.
(888) 934-0888 ext. 3
www.wheatmark.com

ISBN: 978-1-60494-164-7
LCCN: 2008933780

*This book is dedicated to
the glory of God
and to
Parkwood Baptist Church,
Gastonia, N.C.,
Pastor Jeff Long, and all the congregation
who have encouraged me, inspired me, and supported me
all forty-five years of their existence as a church.*

Introduction

The title given to this book may seem to some folks to be a very brash question, and to a few it could possibly appear to be almost blasphemous.. Nothing could be further from the mind and intent of the author. There are probably very few who read this book who have not at some time or other had a thought identical to the words in the title. Virtually every person who earnestly tries to pray will have experienced moments when it seemed as if God were deaf, or at least that He was not listening. Certainly, nothing seemed to be happening. The person praying felt as if his or her prayers were getting no higher than the ceiling.

David must have felt very much that way when he wrote the 13th Psalm. Listen to what he says:

"How long, O Lord? Wilt Thou forget me forever? How long wilt Thou hide Thy face from me? (Ps. 13:1 NASB)

Or note his words in the 10th Psalm: "Why dost Thou stand afar off, O Lord? Why dost Thou hide Thyself in time of trouble?" (10:1 NASB)

Having had that feeling many times with perplexity and frustration, I began to spend more and more time studying God's Word to see exactly what the Author of prayer has to say about this wonderful privilege He gives to those who have faith. This little book is the result of the author's pilgrimage in the path of Prayer. It is my hope that others may be helped as they read it.

In offering this material, in no sense am I saying that I am an expert in the realm of prayer. I am like millions of others who have struggled in the practice of prayer, and have wondered often if, in reality, my prayers were getting through to God. I had no problem recognizing God's ability to hear. I knew full well that he can hear anything He wants to hear. My thoughts were that the problem was with me, not Him. But as I continued to labor in prayer, I so wanted to have the feeling that, whether He actually granted my specific requests or not, He heard my every word. I knew that the answer could not come from experience - mine, or that of anyone else.—but only from God's own Word. I struggled with the question, "Lord, what do I need?" As I searched for the answer, I read many books on 'Prayer.' But the more I read, pondered, studied and sought, the more I realized that the only satisfying answers to all the questions about prayer can be found only in God's Holy Word. For there has been only one true "Expert" in prayer, and that was the Lord Jesus Christ, and the only Divine, totally dependable information is in the Bible.

There are many questions asked about prayer. I have not tried to list them all, obviously. But I thought about those that rose most frequently in my own mind, and sought the answers. What the Bible has given has been a blessing of immeasurable help. In these chapters, I have done my best to compile and organize and provide what I have found to be of great help. I am sure this is not the final word on the subject. Others may do a far better job of ferreting from the Word the truths we need to know. But I offer this as an attempt to be of help, with the hope that those who read it will have a better grasp on the Biblical teaching on Prayer, and will be stronger, more effective 'prayer warriors.' As you read, it is my prayer that you will be blessed and helped by what has been written.

I am convinced that prayer, guided by diligent study of the Bible, is the only means by which spiritual wisdom and growth can be acquired. I am also convinced that the weaknesses of individuals as followers of Jesus Christ are the result of an inadequate prayer life. The ineffectiveness of many of our churches likewise is due to a tragic lack of earnest, agonizing prayer on the part of church members. At the same time, many of those who earnestly pray are, like Lot of old, tormented in soul, "from day to day by seeing and hearing (the) lawless deeds" of our sin-sick society. We cry out to God for help.If we are to have a revival of spiritual power, which is so desperately needed in our part of the world, then earnest, fervent, Spirit-directed praying is essential. It is my prayer that this little book may be useful in helping to bring about that stirring of God's Holy Spirit in the midst of those who know God in Jesus Christ.

There are no shortcuts, and no easy answers. Learning how to pray is a pilgrimage of faith and persistence. One of God's most important instructions is, "Wait on the Lord; be of good courage, and He shall strengthen your heart; wait, I say, on the Lord" (Psalm 27:14 NKJV).

This study of Prayer is divided into three sections. The first is "Facts to Face," – a look at prayer as a concept ; the second is "A Good Look At Prayer"; and third is, "What Makes It Work?"

Contents

Section 1 – Face to Face   1

1. What Is Prayer? 3
2. Does Prayer Really Work? 15
3. Why Should I Pray? 22
4. False Concepts of Prayer 40
5. Hindrances to Prayer 48
6. The One Who Hears 57

Section 2 – A Good Look at Prayer   63

7. Is Attitude Important? 65
8. What Must I Believe? 73
9. What Are the Rules? 81
10. What Is Intercessory Prayer? 92
11. Is Church Necessary? 101
12. What Can I Ask? 108

Section 3 – What Makes It Work?   117

13. Trust and Loving Obedience 119

14. In Jesus' Name 124

15. Staying With the Bible 133

16. Persistence in Prayer 140

17. Depending on the Holy Spirit 146

18. Sharing in the Kingdom of God 154

About the Author 163

Section One – Face to Face

A look at prayer as a concept:
1. What Is Prayer?
2. Does Prayer Really Work?
3. Why Should I Pray?
4. False Concepts of Prayer
5. Hindrances to Prayer
6. The One Who Hears

One

What Is Prayer?

THERE ARE SKEPTICS, AND perhaps some who are simply ignorant, who say that prayer is nothing more than a subjective experience. According to this concept, prayer accomplishes nothing except perhaps to calm and allay the innate fears of the person praying; it is only a subjective exercise and experience of the mind. These skeptics say there is no such thing as an answer to prayer from an outside source of power. They insist that its value lies in whatever inner feeling of benefit it may produce. Those who hold to this idea say, "If you think it helps you, then use it, but don't expect any miracles." Those who have this concept of prayer would likely say that praying for healing is foolish - a waste of time. They do not believe in miracles. Healing, for them, is a part of nature's normal activities, and so prayer can have no effect.

But it is hard to imagine there is a person anywhere who does not, at least secretly, wish there were some outside power into which one could plug to get help in time of urgent need. True believers in Jesus Christ know without a question that He was an ardent advocate and practitioner of prayer. He spent a great deal of His time in prayer. He taught His disciples to pray. His counsel to all who believe in Him was

"Ask, and it shall be given to you; seek, and you shall find; knock, and it shall be opened to you" (Matt. 7:7 NASB). And even though many questions may arise in our minds, we have the conviction that prayer is the line of communication with God, and it is imperative that we learn all we possibly can about prayer. We believe, and seek to follow what Jesus taught.

The Bible clearly teaches that Jesus expects those who believe in and follow Him to pray. He began His instructions to those first disciples by saying, "When you pray ... ." (Luke 11:2). He knew they would pray in some fashion. His teaching had in view the truth "that men ought always to pray ... ."(Luke 18:1). He plainly showed them that prayer is the line of communication with God.

But what are we talking about when we use those words 'pray' and 'prayer'? Everybody knows that 'to pray' means you are asking somebody for something. Is there more to it?

An ancient definition tells us that prayer is the "ascent" of one's mind and spirit to God. Another has said that prayer is the "lifting of heart and mind and will to God." Philip Brooks wrote "A prayer in its simplest form is merely a wish turned Godward." The Westminster Catechism puts it well, "Prayer is an offering up of our desires unto God, for things agreeable to His will, in the name of Christ, with confession of our sins, and thankful acknowledgment of His mercies." Archbishop Francois Fenelon further helps us with these words, "The true prayer is that of the heart, and the heart prays only for what it desires. To pray, then, is to desire – but to desire what God would have us desire."

A beautiful definition of prayer in its simplest form is "A baby crying in the night, a baby crying for the light, and with no language but a cry." For prayer is surely the heartcry of a human being reaching out, even in wordless groanings, in communication to whatever God he or she believes may or does exist. It is a universal impulse. All people pray at one time or another - they cry out to whatever power they feel exists out of and beyond themselves. Even an atheist, in a moment of great crisis, will likely cry out for some hoped-for power outside of and beyond himself.

Christian prayer, in its definition, builds on this simplest universal concept. It is, of course, much more, and on a very different level. It goes far beyond the rudimentary dim groping after some hoped-for Being or power. Prayer, for the person who believes in Jesus Christ as the Son of God and Saviour, is rooted in the conviction and awareness that the God to Whom we pray is a Father God who is all-wise and all-powerful and who has been revealed to us in Jesus Christ as Love and Light. To believe that He is a God who actually loves us opens wide the door for communication with Him. That openness is more than permission. God wants us to pray; He expects us to pray; indeed, through Jesus He instructs us to pray; He is never irritated by our prayers.

Dr. Theodore Adams, for many years pastor of the First Baptist Church, Richmond, Va. told of an experience. He had asked his Secretary not to disturb or interrupt him with anything on certain mornings, when he was preparing his sermons, unless it was a real emergency. One morning his wife came to the church with their small son. While she was busy attending to some church matters in which she was involved, the son wandered down the hall and opened his father's office door. Dr. Adams tells that he was instantly aggravated that anyone would disturb him. When he saw it was his small son, he let his voice reveal his aggravation, "What do you want?" he asked with that tone in his voice. The little boy came quickly to his father's side and said in an aggrieved tone, "I just wanted to be with you, Daddy." Dr. Adams quickly lifted the child into his arms and buried his aggravation in the blessedness of love revealed. God is never aggravated by our praying. The Bible helps us to see that prayer at its highest level is a very involved activity. The saying of words, or the inner mental expression of spiritual desire, is not necessarily complicated. But to bring our praying to the level where God makes us know we are heard, and that our prayers are answered, requires a depth of spiritual understanding that is far more than just voicing a request.

The development process of Christian prayer follows somewhat the same pattern as the growth process of communication between a child and the parent. A baby knows no language but a cry, yet a loving parent quickly learns to interpret the varying tones and intensity and thus discern the meanings of the infant's cry. As the child grows older, he or she learns to express needs and desires in specific terms. Then the more mature the child becomes the more communication between parent and child becomes expressions of fellowship, love, understanding, sharing, as well as expressions of need or desire.

Following that pattern, as babes in Christ, we may not know how to pray in any form except as an inner groaning, a cry to God for help. But as we mature in Christ, we learn to ask for the specific blessings we know we need and desire. Ultimately as spiritually mature individuals we learn to talk with the Heavenly Father on somewhat the same level as our Lord Jesus did, and our prayers, like His, are communications of love, thanksgiving, concern, compassion, and fellowship. But one has to explore in both knowledge and experience the teachings of Scripture concerning prayer for the fullness of understanding and blessing to be received. It is tragic that, for many people who consider themselves to be Christians, their concept of prayer never moves beyond asking for things - what is needed or wanted. They are like a baby crying for food or attention. Their relationship to God, at its best, is not too different from that of a child who has funds controlled and administered by a Trustee. If the child wants or needs anything, a request must be made to the Trustee. That request can be formal and without any personal feeling of any kind. It can be done in several different ways - a note, a letter, a telephone call, or a personal word - none of which requires any warmth of relationship. For many people, their prayer life has progressed no further than this; it is simply a means of making request, or begging for, what is needed or wanted. There is little or no sense of personal relationship.

For the Christian it ought to be, and can be, indeed is, totally different. The true Christian is a child of God - a relationship claimed by the person, and acknowledged by God - a Father-God who loves us. Prayer is the means of communication. Much of our praying, obviously, is asking for what we need. We are to pray for our food - our "daily bread." Jesus recognized this to be the situation. But prayer at its highest level is conversation between a loving Father and a trusting, adoring child. While a baby may only cry for food or attention, the mature child holds intimate conversation with the father. The subject matter may include a request for something which only the father can provide, but it may also involve the many things in which the father and the child have a common interest and a common concern. How, then, can we define 'Prayer'? Christian prayer is expressed in a variety of ways, and the Bible records prayer in a number of forms.

Prayer Is a Mystery

Prayer is a mysterious thing - and a mystery whose Author and Keeper is God. The human mind cannot comprehend all that is involved and all that develops conceptually in prayer. We readily grasp the fact that prayer automatically involves some super Being - a God - and ordinary human beings. But to grasp the proposition that the weakest and most despised individual can somehow project a wish, a desire, a plea, or request into the nothingness of space (for want of a better description) and have that desire heard, and perhaps granted and fulfilled by some Super-Being whose actuality can only be conceived by faith, is hard for the skeptical mind to even envision, much less tolerate. And we are well aware that ordinary individuals have difficulty grasping the amazing blessing wrapped up in the reality of prayer.

As long as we are fully aware of the mysterious provision for, and quality of, prayer, we are not likely to take it for granted. It becomes something we approach with reverent hesitancy. There are times, of course, when our need is so great that we cry out with urgency. But in more thoughtful and quiet moments we cannot help but be silenced as we contemplate the very existence of such a privilege of voicing to a Creator God a petition, or question, or expression of amazement with the daringly assumed conviction that our words will be heard by the One to whom they are addressed. It is a mystery we cannot explain, but for which we are eternally grateful.

The mystery is compounded, of course, for those who have little or no faith. But just as the Gospel is a mystery revealed by God the Creator through His Son Jesus Christ, and put in the hands of the apostles who yielded to Him their fealty and fidelity, so 'prayer' is likewise a mystery which God has opened to those who have faith. We do not understand why God should be so beneficent and so generous, but we learn to accept it as a gift of His love and His plan for the redemption of His creation. Through faith, believers learn to spend time with God - learn to wait on Him, and ultimately, to say as did Job, "Though he slay me, yet will I trust Him."

Prayer Is Petition

We have already discussed the fact that prayer in its simplest form is obviously asking for something—'petition'. The root meaning of the word "pray" is "to entreat or to plead." The dictionary defines the word "prayer" as "a supplication; an earnest request." Jesus recognized the need and the place for this in the Model Prayer. A portion of that prayer is worded, "Give us this day our daily bread …" God is fully aware that we have physical needs - food, drink, clothing, shelter, etc. In fact, He knows our needs before we ask. But He expects us to bring our petitions to Him. By this we acknowledge our dependence upon Him as the ultimate source of all things, and our dependence on His generosity, His economy, His mercy, and His grace. David expressed it for all of us long ago, *"For all things comes from Thee, and from Thy hand we have given Thee … .it is from Thy hand and all is Thine"*(I Chron. 29:14, 16 NASB). Whatever is an essential or blessing of life, we are to ask for it. Not only are we to ask for daily bread,but for all the other needs of our lives. Petition is a vital part of prayer. It is, to be sure, the simplest, the most elementary part, but it is, in a sense, the foundation stone upon which all else stands, or begins. Jesus assured His followers, *"Ask, and it shall be given to you"* (Matt. 7:7 NASB). Should the farmer with a barn full of grain ask for daily bread? Yes, indeed! Whatever he has came from God's hand. To ask for "bread" is to acknowledge that God has the power to withhold bread even when a person has a loaf in his hand. To ask God for the things we need, even when one seems to have an abundance, is to humbly acknowledge that all we have, or can have, comes from His bountiful hand.

In a large part of our world famine remains an ever present threat. At any moment millions are on starvation level. And many millions more have only one or two days supply of food. Here in our part of the world, we have become a civilization of towns and cities. The percentage of people in the U. S. who grow any of their own food is small. Most of us are totally dependent on the food processors, the trucks or railroads, and the grocery or food stores. Not many people today have more than a week's supply of food in the refrigerator, cabinets or pantry. It is easy to overlook or ignore the fact that we are so dependent on others. But we should never forget the fact that God can change that situation so easily. If the trucks were to stop running, in two weeks time, many of us would be without food.

We need not feel guilty, then, in asking God for those things we need. The point where so many fail, of course, is that the petitions are only for material and physical needs. Every Christian needs to grow in grace and wisdom to the place where the recognition and desire for spiritual blessings is greater than the petition for the material and physical.

Prayer Is Praise and Worship

Prayer is much more than just asking for God's blessings. It is also a vehicle for praise and worship. In the Model Prayer, Jesus taught that we should begin prayer with an expression of worship, "Hallowed be Thy Name." Every prayer ought somewhere to voice the yearning of the believer's heart for the praise and worship and glory of God. If the glorious Name of our God is honored as it should be then the result will be the establishment of His Kingdom over all the earth. Thus Jesus continued in the Model Prayer to voice the earnest desire, "Thy Kingdom come. Thy will be done on earth as it is in heaven." (Matt. 6:10 NASB). This can mean only one thing - that our God will be acknowledged as God and King of all the universe. His reign will begin in our own hearts. After all, what point in asking for His Kingdom to come elsewhere if it has not already been established in our own lives? To do so is hypocrisy in essence.

It is blindness and selfishness for us to fill our prayers with petitions and requests for God's help if we never say a word asking that His Name shall be lifted as an ensign, and that His Kingdom shall be established everywhere. The closer we are to God the more concerned we will be that His glorious Kingdom shall be in existence and acknowledged over all the earth. We ought zealously to seek ways by which we can praise our God. His goodness is so overflowing; His mercies are so available; His grace is so essential, yet so free. When we read the Psalms, we cannot help but be aware that praise is a dominant theme. Like the Psalmist, we ought to let praise be the motivating force and the theme of our lives, as we say with him, *"Sing for joy to the Lord, O you righteous ones; praise is becoming to the upright"* (Ps. 33:1 NASB). We ought never fall on our knees, or bow our heads in prayer, or lift them up in joy and gladness but that we praise our God for His goodness and mercy, for His blessings and His gifts.

Prayer Is a Way to Discover the Will of God

Prayer is also the means by which we are helped to discover the will of God in our lives. Jesus taught the early disciples to pray, *"Thy will be done on earth as it is in heaven"* (Matt. 6:10 NASB). Once we have come to know God in salvation through our faith in Jesus Christ, the most important and valuable knowledge we can have is to know the will of God for our lives. Jesus told the crowd gathered around him, *"For whoever does the will of God he is my brother and sister and mother."* (Mark 3:35; Matt. 12:50 NASB). Paul wrote in his letter to the Ephesians, encouraging them - even those who were slaves - to be obedient to Christ, *"doing the will of God from the heart"* (Eph. 6:6 NASB). A child who adores his or her parents will make every effort to please the parents. There will be times when this is not the case, but as a rule, this will be true. And that child will be careful to learn what the parent's wishes are.

A dedicated child of God is likewise anxious to know what the will of the Father is. A true Christian will always be concerned to be in the will of God - doing only those things which one is sure are pleasing to the Father. But because of our humanity, and the fact that the flesh is ever a burden to the spiritual life, it is constantly necessary for us to seek to learn what God's will is. It is through the Bible, the Word of

God, that we learn what God desires and requires, but prayer is the means by which God gives to each of us His will individually.

Jesus taught the disciples, by precept in the Model Prayer, and by His own example, to pray, "Thy will be done ..." It is sheer mockery for us to pray for God's will to be done if we are not willing for our own lives to be submissive to His will. Jesus' own personal prayer was *"Not my will but Thine be done"* (Luke 22:42 NASB). Through prayer we can be given the mind of the Holy Spirit as to what God wants us to be and do. It is well to ask God to reveal to us His will for our lives. It is even more helpful to wait on the Lord, in prayer, seeking to feel in our own minds and spirits the direction and instruction God gives.

God does not always tell us in specific words what His will is for our lives, and for the situation in which we find ourselves. But if we earnestly seek to know His will, He will use whatever means are valid to help us know what we ought to do. The surest and quickest way to a vital awareness of His will is through fervent, continuing prayer, with our minds and hearts guarded and guided by the study of and meditation upon God's Word.

Prayer Is Means of Discovering Barriers to God

Prayer, supported by the Word of God, is the most effective way to know those acts and attitudes which have become barriers between us and God. When we have a desire for close fellowship with God, and somehow He seems far away, earnest prayer, instructed by His Word, is the best means available to reveal to us whatever it is that stands in the way. We can be sure it is not God who has moved away. If there are unconfessed sins, they will be boldly outlined on our consciences. If there is an unforgiving spirit, the Holy Spirit will make us aware of where the roadblock is. If there is disobedience, or if rebellion has reared its ugly head, our inner spirit, sharpened and made sensitive through prayer, will bring to our attention where we have gone astray. When the way between us and God seems stopped up, so that somehow we cannot reach Him, prayer is the quickest way to know there is something wrong, and what it is. And it is only through fervent, earnest confessional prayer that the line to God can become freed,, cleaned, clear and made free-flowing once again. We will not discover the problems by our own self-analysis, but if we open our hearts and lives to God in prayer, He will reveal to us where we fail.

Prayer Is Thanksgiving

Thanksgiving is certainly a part of praise and worship, but it is so vital to the Christian that perhaps we ought to set it apart as worthy of individual consideration. Thanksgiving is a dominant feature in the lives of God's people all through both Old and New Testaments. David voiced it for all of us, *"I will give thanks to the Lord with all my heart; I will tell of all Thy wonders. I will be glad and exult in Thee; I will sing praise to Thy name,. O Most High"* (Ps. 9:1, 2 NASB). Paul tells us what we ought to do. He says, *". .pray without ceasing; in everything give thanks; for this is God's will for you in Christ Jesus."* (I Thess. 6:17, 18 NASB).

Gratitude has been called the memory of the heart. It is the song of the soul in the presence of God. Someone has said that the world is made up of two kinds of people - the thankful and the ungrateful. The most discernable and distinguishing difference between them is that those who are thankful are constantly surprised that life has been so good to them, while the ungrateful are often bitter and resentful because life, as they see it, has not given them all they want.

None of us likes a person who has no sense of gratitude. It is interesting to note that in the account of the healing of the ten lepers, Jesus seemed disturbed by the lack of gratitude on the part of nine of those healed. He said, "Were there not ten cleansed? But the nine - where are they? Was no one found who turned back to give glory to God, except this foreigner?" (Luke 17:11-18 NASB).

Thanksgiving to God is always prayer at its best. And prayer is never what it ought to be without fervent thanksgiving to God for all that He is and all that He has done for us in Christ Jesus. With that as the foundation stone, we should have no problem recognizing that life itself, and all the good things we enjoy are gifts from God's hand. It is a blind person indeed, spiritually speaking, who does not find constant reasons to give thanks to God. Indeed, every prayer ought to begin, "Thank You, God, for what You have done for me…"

Prayer Is Not a One Way Talk

It ought to be clear to us that prayer is not merely voicing a need and a request with the hope that Somebody somewhere will hear and answer. Prayer is the basic instrument and means by which we have communication and fellowship with our God. We can come to Him with not only our immediate needs, but with the deepest yearnings of our hearts, and know that He hears and understands. Not only so, but He communicates to us His desires and purposes, and His will and plans, if we are willing to be still and listen.

Olive Wyon has written, "Not only does prayer spring originally from the divine impulse and the divine initiative: the impulse would die out, and the very desire to pray would fade away, were it not that secretly God continually renews the spirit of prayer in our hearts"[1]

The sounds from a small baby are all one way communication. As long as the infant is crying, or whimpering, the mother or nurse or caretaker has little chance of getting a message through to the child. Only when the infant is quiet can the mother speak those comforting, assuring words needed to bring a sense of well-being. It is only as the child grows that two way communication between the two becomes effective. In the same way, virtually all of the composition of 'prayer' as a line of communication between those who are "babes in Christ" and God the Father is a one way proposition. But as the Christian grows in faith, wisdom, knowledge and understanding, there is more and more time spent in listening as God speaks. Reading God's Word and listening as God speaks by His Spirit, quiet meditation on the things of the Spirit, and humble waiting on God to convey His message —all these are means of rich blessings as we learn to let God take part in our prayer time, instead of merely listening while we tell Him all we want Him to know about our needs.

The New Testament uses several terms for 'prayer":- petition, supplication, intercession, thanksgiving, praise, requests – all of them directed to God and to God only. In simplest language, prayer is talking to and with God. It is the expression of any message we desire to communicate to our God. The marvel is that whether it be the word-

---
[1] Olive Wyon: The School of Prayer, Westminster Press, Philadelphia, 1944.

less cry of a "babe" in Christ, or the deepest yearning of a mature "saint" for the Kingdom of God to become a present reality, God hears and understands. He does not neglect His children, nor turn a deaf ear to their cries. He is always attentive when we pray according to the instructions given in His Word. Apart from our salvation, prayer is the greatest privilege and blessing we have.

Two

Does Prayer Really Work?

ALL RELIGION IS AN exercise of faith in some deity. Prayer is an expression of that faith. Unbelievers obviously scoff at the very idea of prayer, because they deny the reality of any god. They laugh at what they say is the naivety of religionists - those who still believe in a god of some sort. But those who have true faith and know that prayer is a gift from God are not bothered by the skeptics and their scorn.

Yet for those who are still searching, there may be the question - Is prayer for real? Is there reality to the concept? Does prayer actually work? Or, is it only an illusion? Is it an activity justified by results, or is it prompted only by imagination and wishful thinking? Those who are skeptical may argue that prayer is like asking for the moon. The ardent atheist may even say that prayer is a total waste of time and effort, - an essay in futility, a witless speaking into an empty canyon from which an echo may return, but it will still be but the reverberation of one's own words. Such is the thinking prompted by unbelief. The person who is earnest in seeking after God will surely not pay any attention to such skepticism

Faithful believers know that prayer is a blessed reality. It is not an empty, fruitless crying in the night. When the dark night of heavy burden, the blank walls of seeming failure, or the deep anguish of an aching, grieving heart envelop one's life, prayer is the only avenue that brings one to hope. There are many reasons to say that prayer is, indeed, for "real".

Prayer Is a Universal Activity

Wherever one may go in the populated areas of the earth prayer will be found as a natural part of life. Cross into the Muslim world and there prayer is exercised faithfully five times a day. The religion of Buddhism is actually a religion without a god, yet wherever it is practiced, prayer will be found as a regular activity. Wherever there are people, prayer will be found in some form. Archeologists and historians, in their search for information about past civilizations and ancient peoples, have never found a record in which there was no trace of religion and prayer. It is, without question, a cosmic need and a universal experience. Wherever there is religion, there is prayer.

The biblical writers, in their accounts of the nations surrounding Israel, and then of the infiltration of pagan religions into the life of Israel, tell us that every religion mentioned put prayer of some sort at its center. The most spectacular evidence is the confrontation between the prophet Elijah and the prophets of Baal on Mount Carmel. There the prophets of Baal "called on the name of Baal from morning until noon saying, "O Baal, answer us" and that continued until the time of the offering of the evening sacrifice (Cf. 1 Kings 18:26, 29).In contrast, when Elijah's time came in that confrontation, this man of God simply prayed, *"O Lord…today let it be known that Thou art God in Israel…"*(18:36 NASB).

In the various religions of the world, prayer takes many forms. It may involve frantic physical activity, just the fingering of prayer beads, or it may be marked by total silence. Some who pray fall on their faces prostrate; others kneel; still others lift their hands heavenward. Regardless of the physical position, and the manner of expression, and the god that calls forth their faith, people of the world – all nations, all religions, rich and poor, educated and ignorant, old and young – all pray in some way. Of all human practices beyond those required for life, prayer is the most universal. It is found in the most unexplored areas of the world, and in the center of the largest cities – indeed every where people are found.

People Never Outgrow Prayer

Skeptics contend that prayer is a hangover from primitive times. But all evidence affirms the fact that people never become too educated, or sophisticated, to feel the need for prayer. Regardless of the cultural or intellectual level one may reach, prayer may be regarded as essential. A visit to the most primitive groups existing reveals that they feel keenly the need for prayer, and are constantly involved in some form of petition to the god they worship. Go to the opposite extreme, and look at the highest level of intellectual and cultural advancement, and you will find men and women who pray habitually. Indeed, evidence seems to indicate there is more prayer among the highly educated than among those on a lower intellectual level. Mankind, advancing educationally and intellectually, does not outgrow the felt need to pray.

Wherever we find any record of the activity of prayer in the Bible, it is always the most intelligent, and the most cultured who lead the way. Those who are the prime examples of men and women who pray, as recorded in the Bible, are those who are the leaders - those who would be the most likely to be skeptical, and who would be the first to say, "It doesn't work" if, indeed, it did not.

The same is true today. Virtually every President who has served our nation has called on the people to pray. Among the most highly educated and cultured in our land, there are those for whom prayer is an essential. And among the least educated, prayer is likewise a basic part of life.

The urge to pray is more than begging for help. There are days when the joy in living is so full one must give expression. Even those who do not believe in our Christian God, know that the blessings they experience come from beyond themselves. There are times when the beauty and wonder of the world call for an expression of thanks.

Prayer Is Unlimited in Performance

Prayer is the highest form of spiritual activity in which a person can engage. Samuel Coleridge said, "The act of praying is the very highest energy of which the human mind is capable." The marvel is that the quality of prayer is not determined by the words one speaks. It does not matter whether one's vocabulary is confined to only the simplest words, or has expanded to the range of a dictionary, God is not limited, nor expanded, in His actions, by the words we are able to use, nor is His response determined by one's fluency, or lack of it. Jesus made it plain that one is not heard for his or her 'many words' (Cf. Matt. 6:7).

God is so gracious and good in that the effectiveness of prayer does not depend on the level of intelligence, or the educational advancement, of the person praying. Jesus said, *"…unless you are converted and become like children, you shall not enter the kingdom of heaven"* (Matt. 18:3 NASB). If entering the kingdom of Heaven requires the simplicity of a child, surely prayer need not be more complicated or difficult, but is adaptable to childlike faith.

Prayer can be as diverse in form, and as different in expression, as the multiplicity of needs and desires which can be voiced. Persons can pray crudely, ignorantly, even bitterly, using the simplest words in a language, but in those same simple words the most devout and powerful praying can find its way.. Those who are gifted with words may be poetic and erudite in their utterances, yet have their words fall vacantly to the ground, or in the same splendor of expression their praying may be intelligent, deeply spiritual, magnanimous and powerful with God. The quality of a prayer does not depend on its verbosity, or the beauty of its form. Prayers will be as varied as personalities, and as infinitely diverse in spiritual quality. It is wonderful to know that the quality and effectiveness of prayer is not dependent on the words that are used.

Jesus' Teaching and Example

Jesus is the supreme example of how people ought to live. The Scriptures tell us often that He went alone to pray. *"And after He had sent the multitudes away, He went up to the mountain by Himself to pray, and when it was evening, He was there alone"* (Matt. 14:23 NASB). (Cf. Matt. 26:39; Mark 1:35; 6:46, 47; Luke 11:1; John 17). His prayer life so impressed the disciples that they asked of Him, *"Lord, teach us to pray"* (Luke 11:1). His instructions to the disciples were clear, *". .that men always ought to pray, and not lose heart"* (Luke 18:1 NKJV). His warning words to His disciples were often "Watch and pray …" Pondering the fact that Jesus, as a human being, was also the divine Son of God, one might wonder, "Why should He have to pray?" A careful study of what we are told about Him in the New Testament leads us to realize that it was His humanity which necessitated His prayer life. His most passionate praying was done just before His confrontation with the Jewish authorities and His crucifixion. It is apparent that He prepared His way for every opportunity, task and responsibility with ardent prayer. If such prayer was a necessity for Jesus Christ, how much more essential it is for the believer who would know God and live a life pleasing to Him.

Even a cursory reading of the New Testament makes it plain that prayer is a vital part of the Christian faith. It is not something merely added on, but rather, is the very heart of our worship, and the central factor in the relationship between God and those who believe in Him. Without prayer there is no communication with God, and no strength for tasks and responsibilities God would have us assume.

Prayer Is Real

Prayer is not an activity of the imagination. Nor is it merely a ritual in which one engages out of habit. It does not require a designated place, a set position, nor prescribed words. Prayer is the very essence of the spiritual life. Millions of Christians will bear witness to the fact that for them prayer is as 'real' as the air they breathe. Just as a person grows in the skill of communication from the babbling of an infant to the mature and meaningful words of an intelligent adult, so the Christian learns how to communicate with God. The first efforts at prayer may be no more than a cry rising from the depths of one's being when one cannot put into words the anguish of a heartfelt need.

A new, or immature Christian's first prayers may be much like the cry of a baby when hungry, or in need of attention. But as one grows in grace and wisdom, and in the knowledge of our Lord Jesus Christ, one also grows in an understanding of what prayer is all about, and thus learns how to communicate with a Father God whose Holy Spirit becomes our Teacher. True prayer has a hold on eternity, and thus is far more real than the flesh out of which it rises. Without prayer, the Christian faith is a mere philosophy with little, if any, compensation.

God Always Answers

God is not deaf, nor is He inattentive when we pray. He does not grant every request we make, but He hears and answers in His own wise and wonderful way. Sometimes His answer is "No," but if so, it is given from a heart of love and wisdom. Full trust in God accepts even His "No" as the best possible answer.

In God's instructions through Moses to the people of Israel, He said, *"You shall not afflict any widow or orphan. If you afflict him at all, and if he does cry out to Me, I will surely hear his cry"* (Ex. 22:22, 23 NASB). In Ex. 2:24, we are told, *"So God heard their groaning"*. Paul tells us that he prayed three times and asked God to remove his "thorn in the flesh." God did not grant his request, but He certainly heard him, for Paul tells us, *"And He said to me, "My grace is sufficient for you, for power is perfected in weakness""* (2 Cor. 12:9 NASB). God had something of much greater value to give Paul than physical healing at that point.

It is important for us to remember that God is not operating a 'catch-as-catch-can fishing venture'. He is a loving Father-God who made us in His own image spiritually, who loves us, and who wants the very best for His children. God is LOVE. If you know a person loves you, do you not trust that person? The greater that love is, the more completely you can trust the person. God's love is perfect - totally unselfish, self-giving, acting in perfect wisdom and complete knowledge. We can trust Him completely. So when we pray, if our prayer is sincere, earnest, humble, and in faith, then we can afford to wait on the Lord for His answer. And whatever that answer may be, it is the best answer possible. But we can be sure of one thing - God never turns a deaf ear when His children pray.

We do not know who wrote the 91st Psalm, but it sounds much like David. Regardless of the one who penned it, God speaks in it to say, *"He will call upon Me, and I will answer him; I will be with him in trouble; I will rescue him, and honor him"* (91:15 NASB).

Jeremiah tells us that while he was still imprisoned and carefully guarded, God spoke to him saying, *"Thus says the Lord ... 'Call to Me and I will answer you and I will tell you great and mighty things ...'"* (Jer. 33:2, 3 NASB). And God spoke through Isaiah, saying, *"It will also come to pass that before they call, I will answer, and while they are still speaking, I will hear"* (Isa. 65:24 NASB).

Note the marvelous promises and assurances in Jesus' words, *"Ask, and it shall be given to you; seek, and you shall find; knock, and it shall be opened to you."* (Matt. 7:7 NASB). Do we need any other encouragement to pray? His promises are made in those words, "it shall be given to you", and "you shall find," and "it shall be opened to you."

The pragmatic person may still ask, "But does it work? If I ask for something will God give it to me?" The answer to that is "It all depends on a number of factors which will be discussed in the rest of the book. " However, Christians of all denominations, all ages, all races, all nations will testify vigorously that God does, indeed, answer our prayers. He does not grant every request, regardless of our holiness, need, or persistence. But He hears us, and if His answer is "No," in His wisdom that is the best possible response.

Three

Why Should I Pray?

THE CHAPTER TITLE MAY seem like a foolish question. Isn't it obvious that the reason one prays is to receive whatever it is one requests? If I pray for healing, then that is what I hope will be given. One may assume there are few real Christians who would say that prayer is not a vital and important part of life for them. Unfortunately, there are many nominal Christians who simply do not make prayer an essential element in their daily lives. For one reason or another, they apparently give a very small portion of their time and energy to prayer. That is especially true of those who feel that their prayers are not being answered as they desire.

Why should you pray? If you believe there is a God who hears and answers prayer, is it sensible to ignore that fact? God's Word teaches that prayer is an essential activity for those who claim Jesus Christ as their Saviour and Lord. But in the time_conscious, and activity burdened life in which we live, it is so easy to relegate prayer to the back-burner, on the lowest setting. It should not be so. There are many reasons why we should make prayer an essential part of our lives.

It cannot be stated too often or too emphatically that there is nothing more important in the life of the Christian than prayer. That importance is headlined with startling and powerful force by Paul in his Ephesian letter. Note what he says, *"With all prayer and petition pray at all times in the Spirit, and with this in view, be on the alert with all perseverance and petition for all the saints"* (Eph. 6:18 NASB). If I may be so bold as to paraphrase those words, I believe Paul is saying, "Pray at all times in the Spirit with every form of prayer and supplication; to that end, keep alert with continual perseverance, to make supplication in behalf of all the saints." If we take Paul's words seriously as to their meaning, our reaction should be to say firmly, "I must pray. I must put all my heart with all my energy into prayer. Whatever else I may do, I must pray, for it is unquestionably God's will."

To those who seriously question the effectiveness of prayer, the question "Why should I pray?" may be pertinent. Some might quickly answer in the negative. It may appear to them that prayer, in their experience, does not accomplish much, and so they see no reason to spend time in prayer.

There are probably some people who would reply to the question by saying, "The reason I pray is to ask for what I want and need. The Bible says, "Ask, and you shall receive," and so I pray hoping I can get what I want." Others might answer, "I pray because I think it will help me be a better person." Still others might respond saying that prayer helps people get things done - it is an energizing force.

These may seem reasonable answers, but they miss the point. Though it may be true that prayer accomplishes those objectives, the basic purpose of prayer is not stated in any of the answers. God surely wants each of us to be a better person. He wants to give us His richest blessings. And through prayer great things are accomplished. But all of these together do not reveal the reason God has given us the privilege of prayer. Jesus taught His disciples to pray, by precept and example. God's Word clearly reveals that God expects His people to pray. But if we would fully understand why we should pray, we must find out what God means by prayer, and the objectives for which prayer is designed in God's plan.

1. Prayer Is Essential in God's Order and Economy

Note Paul's use of the word "all" in the verse quoted from Eph. 6:18. He says, "with ALL prayer," "at ALL times," "with ALL perseverance," and "for ALL the saints." What a tremendous inclusiveness is expressed. The very immensity of Paul's exhortation illuminates the importance of the subject. The Apostle's call for prayer is emphasized in the words, "be on the alert," or as it is expressed in the KJV, "watching thereunto," for in the Greek text the basic meaning is "being sleepless thereunto." It would have been difficult for Paul to have stated the matter in any stronger language than in the words he used. On another occasion, he made his point with equal emphasis, *"pray without ceasing, in everything give thanks; for this is God's will for you in Christ Jesus"* (1 Thess. 5:17, 18 NASB).

Paul's exhortation in the Ephesian letter follows immediately after his instructions concerning the six pieces of equipment which are the whole armor of God. He is not thinking of prayer as another weapon, but is informed and convinced by the Holy Spirit that it must be the energizing force in all we accomplish spiritually. Most Christians pray SOME of the time, with SOME prayers and SOME degree of perseverance for a small portion of God's people. But God is saying through Paul that we are to be prayerful all the time. That does not mean living on our knees, nor mumbling a prayer constantly. But it does mean we are to be in the spirit of prayer constantly – that wherever we may be, and at any given moment, we have no problem lifting up to God our thanks or our petitions. And it means we are to use all forms of prayer – not just petitions, but every form of supplication and communication to our God. We are to be diligent in perseverance – to be on the alert always, as good soldiers, not to give up or fall asleep at our post. And we are to make supplication for all the saints – all of God's people. That appears an impossibility. But we are to be as concerned as we know how to be for all God's kingdom – all His people everywhere. It is an obvious impossibility for us to know all the places where Christians are, much less knowing the individuals. But God knows our limitations better than we do. If we pray for those whom we do know, then surely God does not expect more. If our minds and hearts reach out as best we can, then we will be doing what our Lord expects of His followers. Paul declared to the Thessalonians that *"this is God's will for you in Christ Jesus"* (1 Thess. 5:18 NASB).

2. Prayer Is Essential to the Kingdom of God

We are not completely selfless when we make that statement. As children of God we have a very personal and vital interest in the kingdom of God. Even as we pray to bring honor and glory to the Heavenly Father, we must also pray for ourselves and our spiritual needs. In that same way, prayer is vital to the well-being of our fellow Christians. Their strength and security depend to a large extent on the prayers of other Christians. Paul continues his exhortation in Ephesians to include his own needs. He adds, *"and for me, that utterance may be given to me, that I may open my mouth boldly to make known the mystery of the gospel … that in it I may speak boldly, as I ought to speak"* (Eph. 6:19, 20 NASB). In writing to the church at Philippi he assures them, *"And this I pray, that your love may abound still more and more in real knowledge and all discernment, so that you may approve the things that are excellent, in order to be sincere and blameless until the day of Christ, having been filled with the fruit of righteousness which comes through Jesus Christ, to the glory and praise of God"* (Phil. 1:9_11 NASB). This is the kind of intercessory praying which is essential to the upbuilding of the kingdom of God, humanly speaking.

For those who truly seek the Kingdom of God and its total establishment, prayer is imperative. We pray for our own spiritual growth and effectiveness as witnesses for Christ, and we pray for our fellow-Christians in the spirit and for the purposes Paul suggests.

3. A Living Faith Depends on Prayer

There are many other reasons which could be marshalled for the claim that prayer is important, indeed, essential. We take note of a few that are paramount in their truth and value. All of these are reasons from our human viewpoint.

First, a living faith cannot exist without prayer; nor will prayer ever be exercised without a faith of some sort. Genuine prayer and a living faith are inseparable. Martin Luther said, "Faith is simply prayer." That may be simplistic, but it is true. A living faith will constantly express itself in earnest, fervent prayer. In 1 Thess. 5:17, Paul exhorts, *"Pray without ceasing"* Common sense tells us he did not mean we ought to stay on our knees twenty-four hours a day. But, as stated earlier, we who know Christ as Lord and Savior, ought to live in an attitude and state of prayer. Paul knew the value of prayer, and depended upon it for his own inner strength. He also coveted the prayers of fellow Christians, knowing their prayers would help him to be the witness the Lord wanted him to be. Continual prayer is essential to faith—even for its maintenance, and especially for its growth. Those who are closest to God are there because they spend much time in prayer. Without prayer, one's spiritual vitality quickly dwindles and disappears. Satan does his best to keep us from praying. Prayer for the Christian has the same sort of essentiality that practice has for the musician, or the athlete. A great pianist is reported to have said, "If I fail to practice for one day, I can tell the difference. If I fail to practice for three days, the audience can tell the difference." The Christian who neglects prayer will quickly find the priorities of life changing. To keep one's focus on Christ and His Kingdom, prayer is essential.

4. Prayer Was Important to Jesus Christ

We have mentioned this before, but it cannot be emphasized too much. In Luke 6:12 we read, "And it was at this time that He went off to the mountain to pray, and He spent the whole night in prayer to God." (NASB) One cannot read the gospels without being made aware that Jesus depended on prayer as the channel for strength and wisdom in His mission and ministry. It was essential to the relationship He had with the Father, and to the life He lived, as well as to the ministry which He gave to the world. You might ask, "Why would this One who was God need to pray?" The answer, of course, points to the true, full humanity of Jesus. He was God incarnate – in the flesh. That is far beyond our ability to comprehend. He had emptied Himself of His deity, (Cf. Phil. 2:7, 8) in order that He might become one of us. Although He was fully the Son of God, He was also fully human, and His very humanity made prayer essential. He was subject to all that confronts us – temptation, weariness, loneliness, hunger, thirst, grief, pain, frustration, anger, and whatever else a human being might experience. It was through prayer that He stayed in such close touch with His (and our) Father in Heaven.

The words 'pray' and 'prayer' are used more than two dozen times in connection with the teachings and activities of our Lord. Prayer, for Him, was not optional, or spasmodic; it was the most vital factor in His life and ministry. If we are to "follow" Him, and be like Him, prayer must be a vital, dominant part of our lives. He not only commanded us to pray; He set the example for us.

5. Prayer Is Key to God's Grace and Mercy

All human beings need the mercy and grace of God. When a true crisis develops even the agnostic will almost automatically cry, "Oh, God!" Unfortunately, there are so many people who know nothing of the blessings God would like to shower on them. They may cry out for help when they face a critical situation, but they are totally unaware of God's love, and His mercy and grace, providing rich blessings at all times.

True Christians, however, are fully aware that constant mercy is what we need, and continuing grace is what we must have if life and effort are not to end in frustration and failure. The writer of Hebrews gives us the wisest counsel we can find, *"Let us therefore draw near with confidence to the throne of grace, that we may receive mercy and find grace to help in time of need"* (Heb. 4:16 NASB). How do we draw near to that wonderful "throne of grace?" Those words declare both God's sovereignty and His compassion. He reigns as King of kings, but His essence is love, which expresses itself always in full compassion. It is plain that God has appointed a way by which we are to seek and obtain grace and mercy. That way is through Jesus Christ our "great high priest." But it is in prayer that we approach that throne. We can lift our prayer to the Father because of our faith in Jesus Christ, but it is only through prayer that we can even knock on the door, or enter that gracious Presence.

There is infinite grace available for our needs, for our God is a gracious, loving, compassionate God. But He has so ordered it that only through prayer can we communicate to Him our needs. All of God's grace and mercy is there, and available, but He does not permit us to know those blessings experientially except as we establish communication with Him in prayer.

6. The Apostles and prayer

The apostles, whom Christ chose to become the first building blocks in His Kingdom, and who are the pattern for all disciples, regarded prayer as the most important activity of their lives. When a problem arose in the Jerusalem church, the Holy Spirit led the disciples to the right decision and solution. Deacons, 'servants', were chosen to handle the physical needs of the body of disciples, while the apostles stayed with what they evidently knew to be the most important and valuable use of their time and effort. They said to the church, *"Therefore, brethren, seek out from among you seven men of good reputation, full of the Holy Spirit and wisdom, whom we may appoint over this business … . but we will give ourselves continually to prayer and to the ministry of the Word"* (Acts 6:4 NKJV). That tells us where their priorities were. As those into whose hands had been placed the responsibility for the establishment and building of Christ's church, they knew they were powerless without prayer as their means of communication with the Father God. They knew without question that prayer was absolutely essential to their ministry.

All through the apostles' writings there is a continual emphasis on prayer. Every letter Paul wrote, except Galatians, has instructions about, or references to, prayer. John says plainly, *"And this is the confidence which we have before Him, that, if we ask anything according to His will, He hears us"* (1 John 5:14 NASB). James tells us, *"the effective, fervent prayer of a righteous man avails much"* (5:16c NKJV). Peter tells us, *"But the end of all things is at hand; therefore be serious and watchful in your prayers"* (1 Peter 4:7 NKJV). Jude urges his readers, *"But you, beloved, building yourselves up on your most holy faith, praying in the Holy Spirit, keep yourselves in the love of God"* (Jude 20-21a NKJV). It is clear that the apostles were fully aware of the importance of prayer in the life of the Christian. They had learned their Lord's lesson on prayer. They knew that without prayer we human beings can accomplish nothing of value in the Kingdom of God. They also knew that fellowship with the Father could be a reality only as prayer was a reality for them.

7. No Spiritual Accomplishments without Prayer

Have you ever thought seriously about how God plans and works to get His will done in His creation? We read the Bible and see how God did mighty things among and for His people, and may well have the idea that if God wants anything done He just DOES it, and that's it. There is no question as to whether God can do what He wants, any time, anywhere. He is able. But with the gift and coming of the Holy Spirit, God has chosen another way.

Dr. Robert Cook, who served as President of Youth for Christ International. Vice-president of Scripture Press, and then President of King's College, Briarcliffe Manor, New York, and widely read author in the latter part of the last century, tells that in his years with Youth for Christ, a friend said to him one day, "Bob, you fellows are very busy promoting a program and an organization, and you are doing a pretty good job of it. But you will never achieve what God has in mind for you unless you make prayer frontal, instead of an afterthought."

Dr. Cook replied, "Brother, we are doing more praying than any group I know. We have at least one all-night prayer meeting each week of our conference, and there is an early morning prayer session every day. It is well attended, too."

The friend said, "That is not what I am talking about. Prayer must be frontal – essential as a critical method – instead of an occasionally scheduled activity … Prayer must become your method, Bob, not just a good activity in which you engage from time to time."

Dr. Cook's word to Christians is "Prayer is God's method of getting things done." Paul would agree, for he says, "… *in everything by prayer and supplication* …(Phil. 4:6).

We need to put forefront in our minds that prayer is the way God has appointed for us, as His servants, to obtain and achieve the accomplishments He desires of and for us. The primary reason we experience spiritual barrenness in our lives and work is the lack of prayer. James puts it bluntly, *"You have not because you ask not"* (4:2). The individual Christian will make little progress in the Christian life when there is a lack of regular, earnest prayer. The preacher will see little results from his labors in visiting, preaching, teaching, or whatever he does, if they have not been undergirded with intensive prayer in his own life. His efforts are also greatly hampered when they are not supported by earnest prayer on the part of the congregation he serves. The Sunday School teacher will see little true results in the class - no converts and no spiritual growth - when there is little praying on his or her part, and on the part of the class members as well. Numbers may be gained with secular methods, but power with God comes only through prayer. Churches can make little or no headway against the unbelief, sin, error, and worldliness around us when prayer is not a priority for the body of Christ, asking for the help of the Holy Spirit in combatting the wiles, the weapons, the work of Satan. God surely says to us in the words of the Apostle, "You have not because you ask not."

Spiritual growth depends on a love for, and an understanding of, God's Word, the Bible. When a believer begins to seriously study God's Word there may be many things which are hard to understand. And there are some things we will not understand this side of heaven. However, prayer guided by the Holy Spirit will lead us in our thinking to a greater discernment of the meaning of the writing. The Psalmist prayed, *"Give me understanding that I may learn Thy commandments"* (Ps. 119:73 NASB). And *"Give me understanding, that I may observe Thy law, and keep it with all my heart"* (Ps. 119:34 NASB). True prayer is not a one-way monologue – it is a conversation between two persons – the believer and God. A prayerful attitude as we study His word enables Him to speak to us through His Word and thus give us the guidance we need and seek. Even as we pray, God speaks to us by His Holy Spirit and points us to the way He would have us go. We can never know the fullness of God's revelation through His written Word, but one of God's beautiful miracles is the way He opens to us an understanding of His will and way. We can never exhaust the riches of the Bible for God continually opens to those of faith the treasures of the truth. Prayer is the seismic sounding that points us to those treasures.

8. Prayer Opens Our Eyes to the Blight of Sin

Sin is the cancer that eats away at the very vitals of every civilization. But like cancer, much of the sin of the world is hidden. And like cancer, it is the hidden sin which is the most devastating and destructive. Christians can never understand the cosmic blight and destruction of sin, nor realize how devastatingly powerful it is, except there be continual study and meditation upon the Word of God, and accompanying prayer that is agonizing and continual. One of Satan's greatest weapons is the power of sin to so blind men and women that they do not recognize its true character and nature. It is so easy for us to become anesthetized to the toxin of sin. Using Isaiah's words (Cf. 28:10), it is "a little here, a little there" and soon we are surrounded with evil that we did not foresee. This is Satan's favorite ploy.

The writer of Hebrews tells us that Lot, living in Sodom, *"felt his righteous soul tormented day after day with their lawless deeds"* (2 Peter 2:8 NASB). Yet Lot stayed in the sewerage of Sodom's morals until it was almost too late. Christians in our Western world are so likely to follow Lot's pattern. The only antidote is to develop a consciousness of the awfulness of sin and a parallel sense of guilt with every transgression of the laws and love of God. How can that be accomplished? How can we gain a growing tenderness of conscience, and fully prepare ourselves to offer to God the sacrifice of a broken heart? (Cf. Psalm 51:17; 34:18). It will come only as we contemplate the stern teachings of God's Word against sin, see sin's final work and result on Calvary's cross, then in utter humility and repentance seek God's face in prayer, asking Him to help us as individuals, as families, as communities, as a nation to turn from the wickedness that is destroying us. When we have the proper preparation of mind and heart, our prayer life will dwell more and more on our own unworthiness and the marvelous grace and love of God revealed to us in the gift of His Son our Saviour. We will see the sinfulness of our society, and be constrained to cry out with Jeremiah, *"Now therefore amend your ways and your deeds, and obey the voice of the Lord your God"* (Jer. 26:13 NASB). It will be a cry from a broken heart, seeing the sinfulness of sin.

When we have a desire for close fellowship with God, and somehow He seems far away, we can be sure it is not God who has moved away. Earnest prayer, instructed by His Word, is the best means available to reveal to us what it is that stands in the way. If there are unconfessed sins, they will be boldly outlined on our consciences. If there is an unforgiving spirit, one's prayers will be hedged in by the Holy Spirit until the problem is recognized. If there is disobedience, or if rebellion has reared its ugly head, a spirit sharpened by and made sensitive by prayer will bring to our attention where we have gone astray. When the channels between us and God are stopped up, prayer is the quickest way to know there is something wrong. If, in fervent, earnest prayer, we let God deal with us, then we can know our shortcomings and failures, and do what is required so that those channels can become cleared and free-flowing once again.

9. Prayer Helps in Understanding God's Word

When a believer begins to seriously study God's Word, there may be passages that are hard to understand. In fact, there will doubtless be some things we will never understand this side of heaven. However, through prayer the Holy Spirit comes to our aid, and helps us to discern at least some of the meaning of the Word, thus making intelligent coope-ration with God possible.

The psalmist prayed, *"Give me understanding that I may learn Thy commandments"* ((Psalm 119:73 NASB); and *"Give me understanding, that I may observe Thy law, and keep it with all my heart"* (119:34 NASB). A prayerful attitude as we study God's Word enables the Holy Spirit to open our minds and hearts to the truths of God's Word, and to give us the wisdom we need in understanding what God desires to say to us. Even as we pray, God speaks by His Holy Spirit to show us what it is He would have us do. None of us will ever know the fullness of God's revelation of Himself and His will through His written Word, but one of God's beautiful miracles is the way He opens to us His truths when we study prayerfully. The psalmist could testify, *"I have not turned aside from Thy ordinances, for Thou Thyself hast taught me"* (119:102 NASB). We can never exhaust the riches of the Bible, but as we dig deeper, the richness of its truths becomes ever more apparent.

A pastor who is often called upon to lead in Bible conferences, made this statement as he began his first message, "To prepare for this Conference, I read the Bible portion we are using fifty times, and each time I read it, God showed me something new." Constant, continual earnest study of the Bible is essential for every Christian. But if we seek to mine its wealth by our own intelligence and skills, we will find it barren in places, and often disappointing. A prayerful attitude opens the way for the Holy Spirit to do His wonderful work in opening up the truth and beauty of the Scriptures. Prayer is the seismic sounding that reaches into the treasures to be found in the Word.

10. The Faucet of the Fountain of Joy

John records for us, in 16:24, the words of Jesus, *"Ask, and you will receive, thast your joy may be made full"* (NASB). Jesus is saying that if we want to be full of joy we must pray. Prayer is the faucet that must be opened if we are to receive all the joy God has in store for us. Prayer is essential because we get only what we ask. It is through prayer that God becomes real to us. Prayer brings the power of the Holy Spirit into our lives. And through prayer we are able to rid ourselves of fear and anxiety, and find the peace of God which passes all understanding.

It is, perhaps, not stretching the imagination too much to say that God leans, as it were, over the windowsill of heaven to hear us when we pray so that He might answer and give what we ask in the Name of Jesus Christ. Surely we are foolish when we fail to use what God gives and urges us to receive. Scripture is plain in saying, *"Pray without ceasing"* (1 Thess. 5:17).

11. Is It Wrong Not to Pray?

Is Prayer important? We have looked at the question from the positive side. But there is also a negative side. The Bible not only tells us that Prayer is important, vital, essential, but it also says to us that we may sin in not praying . Sins, according to the Scripture, are of two kinds - omission and commission. A sin of commission is doing what we know to be wrong. John tells us, *"Sin is transgression of the law"* (1 John 3:4). Sins of omission, however, are those which involve failure to do what we know is right - what ought to be done. James tells us, *"To one who knows the right thing to do, and does not do it, to him it is sin"* (James 4:17 NASB).

Many people have the feeling that sins of omission are much less serious than those of commission. The Bible, of course, has much more to say about flagrant deeds of wrong. But there seems to be no difference between the two in the sight of God - both are sins. All sin in its essence is against God. David expressed reality for all of us when he said, *"Against Thee, Thee only, I have sinned ..."* (Psalm 51:4a NASB).

There are many ways in which we may commit sins of omission. We fail to do what we know we ought to do. We postpone doing what should be done immediately. We do the very least possible to "get by" when our consciences tell us the whole should have been done.

But one of the most common, and most serious sins of omission in Christian living is the sin of prayerlessness. There are few, if any, who are not guilty of this at some time or other. There is no real excuse for it. Prayer is open to every believer. Not everyone can preach or teach, or go as a missionary; not too many can give large sums of money; not all can lead in Bible study, or participate in visitation and witnessing publicly—but everyone can pray. Whether it be in the privacy of your own room, or while you busy yourself at work, or joining in the corporate act of prayer in the life of the church—none are forbidden to pray. and the Holy Spirit never turns one away from prayer. The invalid in a wheelchair, or bed-fast, can pray. The person who is shut in and prevented from attending worship services in chapel or church, can pray. The individual who must work while others gather in worship, can pray. God does not fence in His prayer chambers so that only certain ones may enter, nor does He make certain areas sacrosanct so that only there will prayer be heard. There is no place on earth where prayer cannot be lifted up to God. Jesus prayed on the mountainside, while Jonah prayed from the belly of a fish. Nor is there any circumstance in which prayer of some sort cannot be heard.

A preacher invited to lead in revival services in a church in a small town began his effort on Sunday. But on Monday morning, the local pastor met him for prayer then said, "I want to take you this morning to see the most important member of our congregation." They went to a small house and entered. There on a bed was an older woman. The pastor introduced the visiting minister. After the introduction, the lady said to him, "I am praying that many will be saved this week. I have a long prayer list, but I believe God is going to give me a number of them brought to salvation this week." She then said, "Now I want to pray for you." She prayed a fervent prayer. After they had left her house, the pastor said to the visitor, "Her prayers are the greatest power in our church. She is virtually helpless, and has been for a long time, but her prayers are powerful."

Much of the turmoil in our churches today—congregations divided in rancor, pastors fired from their positions, leaders with clay feet, staff members and congregational leaders guilty of moral turpitude, and steadily shrinking membership—is due in large part to lack of earnest prayer. When a pastor yields to immorality, or becomes guilty of financial delinquency, it is an almost certainty that he has neglected his prayer life. It is also a certainty that his congregation has been woefully delinquent in holding him up in prayer. A layman in one of our rural churches voiced this prayer: "Lord, prop us up on our leaning side." All of us need to be propped up on occasion, and often. That is especially true of the Christian leader in today's world. Satan is searching eagerly for opportunities to trip up those who occupy positions of leadership in the churches and Christian organizations. Pastors, particularly, need the earnest prayers of their congregations propping them up where the temptations might be the strongest.

The closer to God one is, the more that person knows the need for prayer. Preaching rarely edifies the prayerless soul. Whenever God works in the life of an individual it is probably in answer to somebody's prayer. Our failure to pray is of vital significance.

The children of Israel had turned away from God to ask for a king. Samuel, the prophet, had rebuked them saying, *"When you saw that Nahash the king of the sons of Ammon came against you, you said to me, "No, but a king shall reign over us" although the Lord your God was your king. Now, therefore, here is the king whom you have chosen..."* (1 Sam. 12:12, 13a NASB). It was harvest time, but Samuel called to the Lord to send thunder and rain. The rain came at a most inopportune time. When that happened, the people then pled with Samuel, *"Pray for your servants to the Lord your God, so that we may not die ..."* (1 Sam. 12:19a NASB). Then Samuel assured the people that, in spite of their sin, he would not be derelict in his duty. He said, *""Moreover, as for me, far be it from me that I should sin against the Lord by ceqsing to pray for you..."* (1 Sam. 12:23 NASB). He was fully aware of the focal point of his responsibility—it was God, not the people. To fail to pray for them was to sin against God.

It may be helpful to analyze prayerlessness as to the reasons why it is so evidently a sin—a sin of omission to be sure, but a sin against God.

1) To be careless and indifferent to prayer is to despise access to God. The greatest privilege we have as Christians is our unhindered access to God in prayer. The door is open any time, anywhere, and for any need. The first symbol provided for the Christian faith was not the cross, nor a fish, but the veil of the temple torn in half and pushed back out of the way by the hand of God Himself. (Cf. Matt 27:51; Heb. 6:19, 20; 10:19, 20). That strange happening announced to mankind that the way to God is open – no intermediary is needed except Christ. He is now the door. The way is open. Prayer, in God's economy, is to be the normal activity of the Christian. Jesus began His lesson on prayer with the words, "When you pray," not "if you pray." Every time we neglect prayer we turn our backs, as it were, on the way of access to God. If a parent told son or daughter, who

Why Should I Pray?   37

lived next door, "Our door is always open to you, at any time," but that child never darkened that door, what would the parent think? They might feel almost as if the child had spit in their faces, for lack of approach would have the appearance of contempt. God would feel the same way were it not for His grace and mercy.

2) To fail to pray is to live in disobedience to the commands of God in His Word. Jesus instructed His disciples, *"Watch therefore and pray always…"*(Luke 21:36). Paul exhorted the Christians at Thessalonica, *"Pray without ceasing"* (1 Thess. 4:17). To the Romans he wrote, *"I urge you, brethren, by our Lord Jesus Christ and by the love of the Spirit, to strive together with me in your prayers to God for me"* (Romans 15:30 NASB). In nearly all of his letters he emphasizes the importance of prayer. It is quite plain that the Lord Jesus did not, and does not, look upon prayer as an option. The Scriptural commands and instructions to pray are not mere requests. Jesus did not say, "I think it would be nice if you prayed regularly." His words about prayer admit of no dissent on the part of those who love and serve Him.

3) To fail to pray is to deprive the Church of Jesus Christ of what it desperately needs. The malaise which eats away at the vitals of the Christian church is due largely to prayerlessness and the lukewarmness resulting. Many of the churches today are pitifully impoverished spiritually. The New Testament does not describe the Christian life as a bed of roses. Rather, it is described in terms of battle and conflict. The enemy is Satan and the forces of evil. There can be no victory against such forces without the necessary power. Prayer is the only means of acquiring that power. When the resources for great living, great victories in the churches and the Kingdom are readily available, and so easily accessible, and then we refuse to use them - is this not sin?

4) Prayerlessness produces a sadly deficient spiritual life. Satan does not worry much about Christians who do not pray. They

are no threat to his rule in the world. Many Christians fail miserably in their prayer life because they look upon it as primarily a physical activity, carried out according to their own ideas. After they have tried and found only seeming failure, they have come to the conclusion that, for them, a satisfying, victorious prayer life is impossible. Their efforts seem fruitless. Victory over the sin of prayerlessness is won in the same way as the victory over sin when we are saved. Salvation is never assured until one comes to know and acknowledge that he or she can do nothing about sin except to trust in Jesus Christ. Only Christ can atone for sin; only Christ can cleanse us of sin; only Christ can give victory over sin. That includes the sin of prayerlessness. The secret to victory is that one's prayer life must be brought under the control of Christ and the guidance of the Holy Spirit. When Jesus is truly Lord of our lives, we have no problem in talking with God. Prayer should be as much a part of life as breathing. There are no real hindrances to prayer except in our own hearts and spirits.

We must be careful, of course, not to put faithfulness in praying in the same category as the "salvation by works" ethic. Praying is not a requirement for salvation, anymore than is baptism. It is a dangerous thing to develop a feeling of well-being and security solely because of regularity in prayer. God does not "flunk" us because of missed praying, neither does He give us 'brownie points' because of rarely missed 'prayer time.' Salvation is not earned through prayer. An open line to God is part of the salvation given to us in Jesus Christ. We are foolish not to use it.

God says to His people, *"Then you shall call, and the Lord will answer; you shall cry, and He will say, "Here I am""*(Isa. 58:9 NKJV). Again He says, *"It shall come to pass that before they call, I will answer; and while they are still speaking, I will hear"*(Isa. 65:24 NKJV). God hears us when we pray. How tragic to miss the boat simply by refusing to get on it.

The only way to be sure of the reality of God is to pray. Atheists and agnostics, and perhaps others, may argue that unanswered prayer is evidence that God does not exist. An unanswered knock on a door does not mean that no one lives there. And an unanswered prayer in no way means that there is no God to hear it. There are many possible reasons why a specific prayer is not granted. Just as *"Faith is the assurance of things hoped for, the conviction of things not seen,"* (Heb. 11:1 NASB) even so, all prayer is a work of faith. Prayer without faith is a work of foolishness. It requires (1) Faith that God exists; (2) faith that he hears our prayers; (3) faith that He is able to grant the request; and (4) faith that He desires to help us. But there must also be the awareness that He has a will of His own, and He does nothing that is contrary to His own will. And His will focuses only on His kingdom and His glory.

With that in mind, let us look at some of the factors the Bible tells us are vitally important in the matter of communication with God.

Four

False Concepts of Prayer

ALL OF US AT one time or another have asked, or will ask, the question, "What is wrong? Why are my prayers not being answered? "And one may even ask, "Why does God not hear my prayers?" In reply, it can be said with all assurance, 'God does hear. He may not answer immediately, or with the answer one desires, but He is not deaf, nor does He deliberately turn a deaf ear.' He always answers. That answer may be "No." But even His silence is His eternal wisdom and grace in action. This is bedrock truth if we are to have any understanding of how prayer works.

A difficulty which needs to be recognized and faced honestly is that one may have a wrong concept of prayer. There are several false concepts that are recognizable, and which effectively interrupt communication between the one praying and the One to Whom prayer is addressed. The powerline between earth and heaven may be corroded by lethargy and selfishness, but it may also be short circuited by clichés and false ideas about prayer, We live in a humanistic day, and often those who seek to pray are tainted with secularism and humanism without being aware of it. Perhaps an even greater difficulty is that there is such a widespread inadequate concept of the place God gives to prayer in His economy.

Martin Luther once said, "I have so much to do today that I cannot possibly get it done unless I spend at least four hours in prayer." People who are tainted with humanism will quickly declare such a statement to be utter foolishness. They will say, "If a man has so much to do, he ought not to waste much time in prayer." Unfortunately, that is the so-called practical viewpoint taken by many church members. They are too busy to spend much time in prayer. They may even recall the story that is told about Dwight L. Moody who once, on board a ship on which a fire had started, was in the bucket line passing buckets of water, when another passenger said to him, "Dr. Moody, you ought to be praying instead of doing that." His reply was, "Friend, I can pray while I work." Paul says flatly, "pray without ceasing." (I Thess. 5:17).

Let's look at some of the wrong concepts and attitudes which close the door to any intimate, personal relationship with God. It is not true to say that most people do not pray at some time and in some fashion. Man is the creature with the upturned face, and prayer is a natural action. But the posture and activity of prayer may mean very little. The four hundred and fifty prophets of Baal "called on the name of Baal from morning to noon saying, 'O Baal, answer us.' But there was no voice and no one answered." (I Kings 18:26). Their petitions continued all afternoon, accompanied by loud cries, and by cutting themselves with swords and knives, but there was no response from their god. Baal was only a figment of their imagination. When people pray to a non-existent god, it is obvious there can be no response. No matter how loud, or how earnestly, or how pitifully they plead, there will be no answer for there is no one to answer. The God to whom a person prays is a totally critical factor. To pray to the one, true God, revealed in Jesus Christ, is a vital factor in prayer.

Unfortunately, many who address their prayers to the one, true God, have mistaken ideas and false concepts of the God they seek, and false concepts of prayer which render their praying totally ineffective. For our own benefit, let's look at some of these.

The most important, and thus the most effective barrier to answered prayer, is the misunderstanding of the basic purpose of prayer. Since God has given us the privilege of prayer, it is certainly essential that we understand what His basic purpose was and is. So many people have the childish idea that God gave us prayer so we could ask for our physical and spiritual needs. James tells us, *"You ask and do not receive because you ask amiss, that you may spend it on your pleasures"* (James 4:3 NKJV). He then adds, *"Do you not know that your friendship with the world is enmity with God? Whoever then wants to be a friend of the world makes himself an enemy of God"* (4:4 NKJV). Those are life-splitting words. The Devil does his best to make us think we can ride two horses at the same time. Jesus says that can't be done. He said, *"He who is not with Me is against Me, and He who does not gather with Me scatters"* (Matt. 12:30 NASB). He also pointedly told His listeners, *"Do not worry about your life, what you will eat, or what you will drink; nor about your body, what you will put on … For your Heavenly Father knows that you need all these things. But seek first the kingdom of God and His righteousness and all these things shall be added to you"* (Matt. 6:25, 32, 33 NKJV). His basic message to those who follow Him is 'Your primary concern must be for the Kingdom of God. If that is the primary object of your praying, then you will not need to worry about the ordinary necessities of life. God already knows you need those things, and they will be provided.'

The sad fact is that there appear to be only a few who make the concerns and progress of the Kingdom their primary object in prayer. Yet Jesus plainly tells us that if our primary concerns are for the material provisions of life we are no different from the Gentiles who do not know God. He said, *"For after all these things the Gentiles seek."* (Matt. 5:32 NKJV).

The clear teaching of the Bible is that the basic purpose of prayer is the establishment and progress of the Kingdom of God, and the desire for God's will to be dominant in our lives, and in the world around us. Praying only for things of less importance is to trivialize one of life's greatest blessings.

A Second false concept concerning prayer is that one needs only a measure of faith to be effective in praying. The Bible specifically tells us that we need to be instructed by and in the Word of God. Put a child in a large general store and tell him to buy what he really needs; are you naïve enough to think that he will actually select those items which are his real and basic needs? Because most of us are immature Christians, God does not turn us loose to ask for whatever we want, or think we need. We need the instruction of His Word if our prayers are to be directed in behalf of that which is really good. Otherwise, like an unsatisfied child begging for those items which seem most attractive, and being denied, we will be confused and unhappy because God does not grant our requests. To pray in the Name of Christ as we are taught to do means we will ask for those things which Christ can approve. How can you pray in His Name if you do not know what it is that He would desire and approve? The Word of God is the only place where that information can be found. The best preparation for prayer is to be steeped in the Word of God.

It seems almost an oxymoron to say that one's effectiveness in praying is affected by one's moral and spiritual condition. Yet there are those who are blind to the fact that unrepentant, unpurged, unforgiven sin closes the door to God. The writer of the 66th Psalm knew that. He said, *"If I regard iniquity in my heart, the Lord will not hear"* (Ps. 66:18 NKJV). Jeremiah tells us that the Lord told him not to pray for sinful Judah, *"… do not pray for this people, and do not lift up cry or prayer for them, and do not intercede with Me, for I do not hear you"* (Jer. 7:16 NASB). Our God is holy. The only time He ever permits sin to come close to Him is when there is a prayer for forgiveness. Then He permits one of His attending angels, or seraphim, to take a burning coal from the fire of the altar where the sacrifices of self are offered and consumed, and with that removes confessed sin. (Cf. Isa. 6:6).

But not only is it brazen sin which bars prayer from the throne of God. There can be no fellowship with God when one has a wrong spirit. The wall which rises in one's way to God is not of His construction. Prayer requires communion with God, and that means there is a mutuality of spirit. When two people have widely different attitudes toward a given subject, real communication is denied. Words may be spoken, but there is no sense of understanding and commonality. Without true fellowship with God, and the open way it provides, prayer is no more than an exercise in futility, a mere mouthing of words. The only prayer that an unsaved person can pray and be heard is "God be merciful to me, a sinner, and forgive me," prayed with a penitent heart. And in reality, that is the only prayer a Christian who is out of sync with God can pray. It is a serious false concept to think that one's spiritual condition is of little or no consequence in prayer.

A fourth false concept is that prayer is more effective if it is phrased in beautiful words, and uttered in unctuous tones. Those who think in this way are also likely to be those who appear to believe they are heard for their 'much speaking.' In this group are those who delight to pray in public so they may be seen and heard. Those who think the composition and delivery of a prayer are most important are generally those who seek to manipulate people..

This is the world's way; it is a fleshly, worldly pattern. Jesus says of such, "Truly, they have their reward." Hypocrites pray to be seen and heard and praised. "They have their reward." They get what they want. But Jesus said to all disciples, *"Do not be like them ..."*(Matt. 6:6 NASB).

The best prayers are the simplest. God is not concerned about the words we use. His concern is for the earnest yearning of the heart and mind. In fact, there are many times when we do not know how to express our yearning in words. The Holy Spirit will take care of that. Paul assures us, *"And in the same way the Holy Spirit also helps our weakness; for we do not know how to pray as we should, but the Spirit Himself intercedes for us with groanings too deep for words, and He who searches the hearts knows what the mind of the Spirit is, because He intercedes for the saints according to the will of God"* (Rom. 8:26, 27 NASB). Paul is saying that if our deepest concern is for the will of God to be done, and we do not know how to put it in words, the Holy Spirit will convey that message to God for us. It is foolishness to think that God requires us to put our thoughts in perfect English, or whatever language we may use. He knows our very thoughts. The psalmist knew that well, *"The Lord knows the thoughts of man, that they are a mere breath"* (94:11 NASB). God Himself spoke through Isaiah, *"For I know their works and their thoughts..."* (66:18 NASB).

A fifth false concept is to think of prayer as a sort of magic formula which, when expressed in exactly the right words, and offered in the right posture, with precisely the right actions or motions, will produce what is requested. There are apparently those who have this notion. Their idea is that if they say the right words the right number of times in the right way, they become a magic formula which works to persuade God to grant their request. What they are seeking to do is to manipulate God – to get what they want whether it is God's will or not. Obviously, God is not a puppet who moves when we pull the right strings.

This misconception has led many to believe that if a person prays long enough and hard enough, and sincerely, God can be moved to do what is asked. Those who hold to such a belief will quote Jesus' parable of the unjust Judge, who said, "*... because this widow bothers me, I will give her legal protection, lest by continually coming she wear me out*" (Luke 18:5 NASB). But Jesus ends that parable by saying, "*Now shall not God bring about justice for His elect who cry to Him night and day, and will He delay over them? I tell you He will bring about justice for them speedily*" (Luke 18:7, 8 NASB). They also like to use the parable of the appeal to the friend at midnight. They delight in the words, "*I tell you, even though he will not get up and give anything because he is his friend, yet because of his persistence he will get up and give him as much as he needs.*" (Luke 11:8 NASB). But it is important to note what Jesus says at the end of that lesson, "*If you, then, being evil, know how to give good gifts to your children, how much more shall your Heavenly Father give the Holy Spirit to those who ask Him?* (11:13 NASB).

Only a childish mind will move in this direction. Mature Christians do not think in terms of trying to wring things from God. True faith is trusting God all the way. It begins with the confidence of being loved, and moves on the premise that God knows our needs better than we do. There is no formula for prayer. God cannot be persuaded by our tactics. He wants to answer our prayers, but He will not be maneuvered by us. He tells us through Isaiah, "*It will also come to pass that before they call I will answer, and while they are still speaking, I will hear*" (Isa. 65:24) NASB).

Perhaps the worst of these false concepts is the belief that if one has enough faith he can always have his prayers answered favorably.

Those who hold to this quickly quote Jesus' words, "*. . if you have faith the size of a mustard seed, you will say to this mountain, 'Move from here to there,' and it will move; and nothing will be impossible to you*" (Matt. 17:20 NASB). – They also quote "*Jesus answered saying to them "Have faith in God. Truly I say to you, whoever says to this mountain, 'Be taken up and cast into the sea' and does not doubt in his heart, but believes what he says is going to happen, it will be granted him. Therefore I say to you, all things for which you pray and ask, believe that you have received them, and they will be granted you*" (Mark 11:22-24 NASB); -- Quoted often also is "*And the apostles said to the Lord, "Increase our faith." And the Lord said, "If you had faith like a mustard seed, you would say to this mulberry tree, 'Be uprooted and be planted in the sea,' and it would obey you.*" (Luke 17:5, 6 NASB)

There is no question as to what Jesus is saying here – 'faith' is requisite for answered prayer. Great faith could move mountains, or replant a mulberry tree – nothing is impossible. But so far as we know, in all these two thousand years since Jesus made those statements, no one has said to a mountain, "Move," and it has moved. One of four things must be true: (1) Jesus was mistaken; (2) No one has ever had faith enough; (3) Jesus was speakingin parabolic terms, or (4) we must misinterpret the word "faith," as He uses it here.

We can be sure Jesus was not mistaken. Paul says of Him, "*…in whom are hidden all the treasures of wisdom and knowledge.*" (Col. 2:3 NASB). And He Himself said "*I am the way, and the truth, and the life …*" (John 14:6 NASB). He never played games with words. We can take His words as face value.

We may be tempted to say that no one has ever had faith enough to make Jesus' words a reality. But Jesus Himself put it on seemingly low terms, "*faith like a mustard seed,*" – in Matt. 13:32 he says of the mustard seed, "*this is smaller than all other seeds. .*" Surely He is not saying that 'faith' is beyond the ability of those to whom He was speaking. The mustard seed analogy would say that 'faith' is in the realm of possibility for any believer, for He added, "nothing shall be impossible to you." Even moving a mountain with a word is in the realm of the possible – but the power is not in faith, it is in God. Jesus said, "The things impossible with men are possible with God." (Lk. 18:27 NASB). Jesus is saying, I believe, that nothing can be done without faith, and nothing is in the realm of the impossible if it is in the will of God. But the faith which is essential is not faith in faith; it is faith in God, and that faith seeks only the will of God.

Jesus was speaking in parabolic terms. Why would anyone ever need to move a mountain, or cause a tree to be uprooted and moved? But if either of those should be in God's will to be done, either could be accomplished by the power of God. Jesus used the same method of teaching when the young man with great wealth came asking, "What good thing shall I do that I may obtain eternal life?" When the interview was over, Jesus said to the disciples, *"It is easier for a camel to go through the eye of a needle, than for a rich man to enter the kingdom of God"* When the disciples asked , "Then who can be saved?" His reply was *"With men this is impossible, but with God all things are possible."* (Cf. Matt. 19:16-26 NASB). Obviously, no faith is going to operate in making a camel go through the eye of a needle, but if it were necessary in God's eye, it is not in the realm of the impossible.

The great problem with many people is that they think in terms of faith in 'faith.' "If I can just have enough faith, I can do anything." Jesus is surely saying in essence, 'It doesn't take a great amount of faith to accomplish God's will. But faith which works is true faith in God and His will.' James put it very clearly, *"You ask and do not receive because you ask with the wrong motives, so you may spend it on your pleasures"* (James 4:3 NASB). True faith in God is that which believes in Him so completely that the whole of one's life is committed completely to His purpose and will. The prayers of such a life need only faith like a mustard seed.

It is hard to imagine that it would ever be part of God's will and purpose for a mountain to be lifted up and cast into the sea, or that a mulberry tree would need to be pulled up and planted in the sea. Jesus is certainly saying that if either of these ever needed to be done for the glory of God, and there was one who had faith to believe it was God's will and thus would be done, it would happen. But He is certainly not saying that if there is anything one of us can dream up and ask, (like literally moving a mountain) if we think we have faith enough, it will take place.

Five

What Hinders Answered Prayer?

WHY ARE MY PRAYERS not answered? If I ask for good things, what keeps God from granting my requests? What gets in the way? If I believe in God, and believe that He is able to answer my prayers, what prevents Him from hearing me, and giving what I ask for?

Those are pertinent questions. God has so much to give us, especially in the spiritual realm. It is tragic not to receive what He is able to give us, and wants us to have. We have discussed false concepts of prayer which put the one praying behind a wall with no doors. To start from a false concept is to be totally separated from God. But there are other perils to prayer as well. Scripture clearly teaches that there are hindrances which we may allow to barricade the way to God.

We do not need to be told that prayer is the secret of power with God. No spiritual heights are reached except when we get on our knees, at least in spirit, in humility before God as we pray. Yet most of us know well the frustration, or disappointment, of unanswered prayer. We know, of course, that Satan is always busy working to put obstacles and hindrances in our way. And, unfortunately, we help him when we yield to his temptations. So it is important for us to know

What Hinders Answered Prayer?   49

something of those facts and factors which may constitute hindrances to our prayers.

James tells us, "You ask, and receive not, because you ask amiss, that you may spend what you get on your pleasures" (James 4:3 NIV). Does that mean God does not want us to have anything that brings pleasure to our lives? No, indeed! But what James tells us is pointed truth. Yet, at the same time, we know there are many earnest prayers which are not selfish in purpose, but which are not answered affirmatively. Prayer is made for a loved one or close friend who is critically ill, or has a severe problem, but no change appears. Paul tells us that three times he pleaded with the Lord to remove the thorn in the flesh which tormented him, but God said, "No." (2 Cor. 12:7-9). Jesus prayed, *"O My Father, if it is possible, let this cup pass from Me."* (Matt. 26:39 NASB). But the answer came back "No," and His acknowledgment was *"My Father, if this cannot pass way unless I drink it, Your will be done"* (Matt. 26:42 NASB). It is essential for us to remember that God is far wiser than we are, and though we believe we have true faith, and know that He may have definite purposes in withholding the answer we desire, we cannot help but wonder if the reason may lie within us and contribute to our seeming failures. And it is obvious that there are attitudes and actions which put roadblocks between us and God. We begin with what James tells us. There surely is no problem in recognizing that a purely selfish motive and purpose nullifies prayer. We may ask for perfectly proper things, even things God wants to give us, but if the motive is wrong, then the prayer is bound to fail. It is imperative to remember that the underlying purpose of all prayer must be that God will be glorified in the answer. Anything we ask only for our own benefit, pleasure or self-gratification simply fails to reach the high plane God requires for prayer to meet His specifications. A difficult lesson to learn is that prayer must not focus attention upon ourselves, but rather must center on God and His kingdom. The Central purpose of prayer is to enable those of us who are followers and disciples of Jesus Christ to share in the extension and building up of His kingdom. When God does not grant our requests, it is not that He is inattentive or angry, but rather that He wants to bless us on a far higher level than we are asking. As an example – a woman prays for her husband to be saved. He is a lost sinner, headed for an eternity without God, living a life totally contrary to the teachings of Christ. It is a proper and highly desirable objective. But what of the motive? Is she praying primarily in order that life may be easier for her? If so, her prayer is basically selfish. For God to hear, and be interested in answering her prayer, there must be two objectives which have priority – first, that God may be glorified, and that His will may be done in her life, as well as in the life of the husband; and second, that a lost soul may be saved from eternal damnation, and Christ be exalted. If those are her real purposes in the prayer, then she may well thank God for the joy that will come in her own life.

It is even possible that prayer asking for the guidance and power of the Holy Spirit in one's life may be selfish and prideful. God is not going to pay much attention to a prayer that seeks to glorify the person asking. When the disciples in Jerusalem heard that the Gospel had been preached in Samaria, they sent Peter and John to give assistance (Cf. Acts 8:14-24). When these two men arrived, they prayed that those who had heard the Good News might receive the Holy Spirit. That prayer was answered in fulfillment, when the Apostles laid hands on those who had believed, and they received the Holy Spirit. In the larger group was a man named Simon, who had practiced sorcery. When he saw what had happened, he appealed to the Apostles, saying, "Give me this power also, that anyone on whom I lay hands may receive the Holy Spirit" (Acts 8:19 NKJV). There is nothing wrong in desiring to have the Holy Spirit resident in our lives. In fact, every true disciple has received the Holy Spirit as God's gift. (Cf. Eph. 1:13, 14) And every believer ought to desire the power of the Holy Spirit working in his or her life for the glory of God. But if the reason is the personal benefits envisioned – happiness, poise, power, etc. – God is not going to be greatly interested in affirming such a desire. The point in all this is that even in praying for something which appears to be totally good, it is possible to be selfish. When one prays for the presence and power of the Holy Spirit (could there ever be anything bad in that?) it must be in order that God may no longer be dishonored by the low level of dedication in one's life, and that one may become fully effective in service to God. When the power of the Spirit is envisioned in one's life, it ought to be with the sole purpose that Christ will exalted, and the kingdom of God brought nearer to its fruition.

It is so easy for prayer to be selfish or egocentric. Strangely, even prayer for revival may be selfish. True revival can bring nothing but good. Surely it ought to be true that any prayer for revival would get God's attention. But when prayer for revival is made, if the thinking is primarily about the church as an organization – its growth, strength, greater prominence and influence, and even warmer fellowship – God Himself is left on the fringe. It is possible to earnestly desire real revival – when souls are saved, and righteousness becomes desirable, but with the hope that the community will be a better place to live – less crime, divorce, delinquency, problems, and a better world – and leave God out of it. To ask for anything in which the answer would fail to glorify God as its priority is to invite failure in prayer. Humanism in any form as the priority is a major hindrance to answered prayer.

A second hindrance to answered prayer is disobedience to God. John tells us, *"And whatever we ask we receive from Him because we keep His commandments and do the things that are pleasing in His sight"* (I John 3:22 NASB). Disobedience closes the door to God. His Word says, *"He who turns away his ear from listening to the law, even his prayer is an abomination"* (Prov. 28:9 NASB). God spoke through Isaiah, *"And when you spread out your hands in prayer, I will hide My eyes from you, yes, even though you multiply prayers, I will not listen"* (Isa. 1:15 NASB). The reason? *"Sons I have reared and brought up, but they have revolted against Me."* (1:2 NASB).

God is holy and righteous. Whatever God touches is either made holy to Him, or is destined for destruction. He is patient and long suffering, but He will have no part in anything sinful. The only prayer He will hear from a sinner is the sinner's prayer, "God, be merciful to me, the sinner."

The essence of that prayer is confession of sin. When the believer permits sin to be resident – staying over a period of time – in his or her life, there must first be a prayer of confession and repentance before any other prayer can be heard. When there is realization that sin is a barrier and a hindrance, one needs to pray that God will make known the sin, so that it can be seen clearly in its ugliness and evil. Then can come the prayer that He will give help in turning loose of that sin or sins in full repentance, so cleansing can come, and fellowship be fully restored. Then the Holy Spirit can rule, and prayer will be heard.

A third hindrance to answered prayer is lack of faith. James tells us, "*... one who doubts is like the surf of the sea driven and tossed by the wind. For let not that man expect that he will receive anything from the Lord, being a double-minded man, unstable in all his ways*" (James 1:6-8). Unbelief is an impassable barrier to God. God requires that we shall believe His Word. To question it to term Him a liar.

For the last two hundred years there has been a systematic and determined effort to generate in the minds of people the concept that the Bible is a humanly written book which God stoops to use on occasion. The argument can be made to sound very convincing. The result is we now have a vast portion of confessing Christians who look upon the Bible as a book which must be judged by human standards. Many of them do not regard the Bible as "God's Word." They may say it CONTAINS the word of God in places, but insist that much of it is myth. Such thinking becomes an existential exercise in which the individual, or at least some individual, assumes the role of judge of the book, to decide which part is divinely given and what is not. Once this concept is adopted, it is easy to disregard, or even eliminate, any portion of the Bible that offends. If a person does not believe in miracles, then all miracles are dismissed with ease; they simply did not happen. Following the German scholar Rudolph Bultmann, one says the accounts of miracles in the Bible are stories used to convey a truth. If one does not believe that a dead person could ever be raised from the dead, then the resurrection of Jesus Christ is denied, or explained away. Such is the cancer of unbelief.

The faith James writes about is not belief that a prayer will be answered. It is an unquestioning trust in the wisdom and goodness of God. James uses Abraham as an example. Abraham believed and took

God at His Word, to the extent that he was willing to obey even when God told him to offer up his only son. Such faith enables one to say, "Thy will be done."

The person who believes in the reality and efficacy of prayer will do all in his or her power to increase in faith. The disciples asked of Jesus, "Lord, increase our faith." (Luke 17:5). We need to pray that same prayer daily. Nothing assists in this more than the consistent reading and studying of God's Word prayerfully, eagerly and expectantly. There is no better way to still the tossing of doubt than to read God's Word regularly accompanied by the prayer, "Lord, I believe; help my unbelief." And again be mindful of the fact that the faith which is essential in prayer is not faith that a specific prayer will be answered, but the willingness to trust God completely with a simple child-like faith.

A fourth hindrance to prayer is shown in Mark 11:25, "*And whenever you stand praying, forgive, if you have anything against anyone; so that your Father also who is in heaven may forgive you your transgressions*" (NASB). An unforgiving spirit is a common hindrance to answered prayer. God will not listen to us when we harbor ill-will or a desire for vengeance against another. A grudge closes the door to God. There must be nothing to hinder communication between a believing, trusting child and a loving Father God. Jesus put it plainly, "*For if you do not forgive men, then your Father will not forgive your transgressions*" (Matt. 6:15 NASB). An unforgiving spirit is an impassable barrier to God.

The answer to this problem, of course, is confession of sin and a willingness to forgive. If you want to know whether you have a right attitude toward someone, try praying for that person. Can you honestly ask God to bless that person? If you can do that, you have no problem. On the other hand, it is wise to keep in mind the words of John, "*If we say we have no sin, we are deceiving ourselves, and the truth is not in us. If we confess our sins, He is faithful and just to forgive us our sins, and cleanse us from all unrighteousness*" (I John 1:8, 9 NASB).

A fifth hindrance is pointed out to us in I Peter 3:7, "*You husbands, likewise, live with your wives in an understanding way, as with someone weaker, since she is a woman, and show her honor as a fellow heir of the grace of life, so that your prayers will not be hindered"* (NASB). He is saying, in reality, that a wrong, or poor, relationship between husband and wife is a hindrance to answered prayer. Why?

God has established that the relationship between husband and wife should be the closest possible – the two are to be as one. When anything disturbs or weakens that relationship, then arises a barrier between them which affects their relationship to God. Peter makes two points – first, the husband, as the head of the home, is to manifest a warm and caring understanding of the woman and her role and her needs. It is his responsibility to take the lead in setting the tone and atmosphere, and establishing the character, of their relationship. Unless there is such understanding and loving agreement, there can be no fellowship in prayer. God surely expects their oneness to extend to, and find its greatest perfection in, their prayer life. Their agreement in spiritual matters is surely covered in that statement of Christ, *"...if two of you agree on earth about anything that they may ask, it shall be done for them by My Father who is in heaven"* (Matt. 18:19 NASB).

If the wife is not a believer, obviously the husband, no matter how devout he may be, cannot share with his wife all the blessings of the Christian life. He can be to her all he ought to be, but if she experiences no participation with him in the spiritual blessings found in Christ, then there is a 'no man's land' between them. So, if one of the two, husband or wife, is not a Christian, the prayer life of the believer, at its best, is not all it could be.

Peter's second point is that the husband is to make his wife know their bond is more than physical. They are joint heirs of the grace of life. They are to help each other in the pursuit of the will of God in their lives. They are both partakers of the gifts of God, and are joined together not only by wedlock, but by a common faith and the hope of a common salvation. Thus, they will help each other in their spiritual pilgrimage. They are fellow travelers with similar needs. In prayer, they will find it easier to recognize the spiritual needs of each other. One of the greatest blessings of the married life is that husband and wife can join in bringing their requests to God.

Wrong or failing relationships in marriage will cause spiritual deadness. A man who makes a pretense in piety, but has no consideration for his wife, is a fraud. So far as his wife is concerned, his prayers stop with the ceiling of the room. Likewise, a wife who may seem to others a paragon of virtue, but who wounds her husband constantly with sharpness of criticism and rebuke, puts a ceiling over her prayers so far as her husband is concerned. He will have no faith in, or patience with, her prayers. At the same time, her attitudes become a barrier to his praying in her presence. Those who have such problems need to humbly and openly confess their failures to each other, and then spread their married life before God and ask Him to put His finger on what is displeasing to Him, and what is keeping them both from the joy they ought to be sharing in a common closeness to the Heavenly Father. Jesus said, "... *if two of you agree on earth about anything they may ask, it shall be done for them by My Father who is in heaven*" (Matt. 18:19 NASB). If there are any two on earth who ought to agree in their prayers, it surely is a loving, God-fearing husband and wife who have a beautiful unity in spirit. They are heavenly blessed.

A last hindrance we mention is failure to be a good and faithful steward of what God gives. Proverbs 21:13 Says, "*He who shuts his ear to the cry of the poor will also cry himself and not be answered*" (NASB). God will not – indeed, cannot – give generously to one who is stingy and selfish. Such a person may accumulate great material wealth, but they will never bless others, and in turn, will never be blessed by what they have. Rather, such wealth will become a burden, and that person will become a burden and a source of great anguish in one way or another. The truth of this, however, is not limited to those with material riches. The poorest may have the same spirit of greed and covetousness which those with plenty may have. Jesus counseled, "*Give and it will be given to you: good measure, pressed down, shaken together, running over, they will pour into your lap. For by your standard of measure it will be measured to you in return.*" (Luke 6:38 NASB). Powerlessness in prayer may often be due to a person's failure to have a generous heart and spirit. The one mighty in prayer is usually a mighty giver.

There are, no doubt, other hindrances to prayer. These we have looked at are the most obvious and predominant barriers. It is both a privilege and a responsibility for each of us to work to remove anything that becomes, or could be, a barrier between us and God when we pray. It is tragic when a person permits anything to prevent God from hearing and answering earnest prayer requests.

Six

The One Who Hears

To whom do you speak when you pray? You probably say "That is a silly question? I talk to God." But the sad fact is that some folks actually are talking only to themselves. Jesus gave the parable of the Pharisee and Publican who went up into the temple to pray. But He says of the Pharisee, "The Pharisee stood and was praying thus to himself"(Cf. Luke 18:11). The truth is – it is easy for us to pray just to ourselves without really meaning to do that. We may be thinking about what words to use, and just what to say.

It is important to know to whom you are talking. That is especially true in the realm of prayer. But it is also vitally important to know the One with whom you converse. In any conversation, your knowledge of the one with whom you speak will dictate in large measure the course of the conversation. Your knowledge of God will be a limiting, or an expanding, factor in your prayers.

The Bible begins with the words, *"In the beginning God created the heavens and the earth"* (Gen. 1:1) . That is a striking statement. It tells us nothing about God except something He did. Nowhere in the Bible does it tell us where God came from, and little about what He is like. One has the feeling that anyone who picks up a Bible and reads it will know that God exists. Yet the whole purpose of the Bible is to tell us about God and lead us to acquaintance with the One who is our Creator.

What is it then that the person who prays ought to know about the One to whom prayer is addressed? Since it is this God who has put into the hearts and minds of His created beings the concept of prayer, we can assume that He hears our prayers. In fact, if we believe Him to be the Creator, then we also may assume that he knows our every thought. In fact, Isaiah records God as saying *"And it will come to pass that before they call I will answer, and while they are still speaking, I will hear"* (Isa. 65:24; Cf. 58:9; Ps. 50:15; 91:15).

What are the attributes of this Person we call God? An ancient creed speaks of God as "a Spirit infinite, eternal and unchangeable in His being, wisdom, power, holiness, justice, goodness and truth." Here are the things we need to know about the God to whom we pray.

He is pure Spirit. Jesus said, *"God is spirit, and those who worship Him must worship in spirit and truth"* (John 4:24 NASB). This is the nature of God. As spirit He can be everywhere. He cannot be seen. John tells us *"No man has seen God at anytime ..."* (1:18 NASB). When you pray to God, He is right there with you, not off yonder in heaven. He knows your inmost thoughts; you don't have to yell at Him. David cried out in amazement, *"Where can I go from Your Spirit? Or where can I flee from Your presence? If I ascend to heaven You are there; if I make my bed in Sheol, behold You are there. If I take the wings of the dawn, if I dwell in the remotest part of the sea, even there Your hand will lead me, and Your right hand will lay hold of me"* (Ps. 139:7-10 NASB). We can never be any place where God cannot hear a prayer and receive our worship. And we can never be physically or geographically beyond God's help when we are in need.

He is eternal and unchangeable. It is beyond our mental ability to comprehend the fact that God has always been – He had no beginning. The Psalmist declared, *"Before the mountains were born or You gave birth to the earth and the world, even from everlasting to everlasting, You are God ... For a thousand years in Your sight are like yesterday when it passes by"* (90:2, 4 NASB). He is as youthful and strong today as when He put

Adam and Eve on their feet. Of Him is said, *"...the heavens are the work of Thy hands. Even they will perish, but Thou dost endure; and all of them will wear out like a garment. ... But Thou art the same, and Thy years will not come to an end"* (Ps. 102:25-27 NASB). Whatever we learn about God from His Holy Word, we can know He is the same today. And He offers to His children the assurance, *"the eternal God is your refuge, and underneath are the everlasting arms"* (Deut. 33:27 NKJV). It is impossible for the human mind to grasp and understand that our God had no beginning, and will have no end. We cannot get outside of the concept of time, but with God there is no such thing as time. He is eternal.

He is an omnipotent God. He is the Almighty, all-powerful One. This name for Him in Hebrew is SHADDAI. A favorite translation is "The God Who is Enough." He is the God who can do whatever He wants to do. He exercises His power according to His own will. He never acts in power except His wisdom decrees it. The things He cannot do are those which His will denies. *"He cannot deny Himself"* (2 Tim. 2:13). He "cannot lie" (Titus 1:2). Therefore *"God cannot be tempted with evil"* (James 1:13). This is divine evidence that Jesus, the Son of God, was fully human, because He was tempted in all points even as we are. At the same time, God has decreed that He will not submit to any test. In reply to Satan's effort to tempt Him, Jesus quoted Deut. 6:16, *"You shall not put the Lord your God to the test."* Satan was quoting prophetic Scripture which applied only to Jesus as the "Son of God." In reply Jesus also quoted Scripture which applied to Him as the Son of Man. Jesus also said, *"With God all things are possible"* (Matt. 19:26). Daniel affirmed *"Our God whom we serve is able"* (Dan. 3:17). The world around us is perverse and threatening, and our hope is that it will be changed. God promises us that it will be changed. He is able to do just that. But He has His own time table and His own ways. With His words of assurance, we can exercise our faith and become part of His plan to make that change.

Our God is All-wise, omniscient. God knows all things, past, present and future. Scripture declares His perfect knowledge. *"There is no creature hidden from His sight, but all things are open and laid bare to the eyes of Him with whom we have to do"* (Heb. 4:13 NASB). Paul exulted,

"O the depth of the riches both of the wisdom and knowledge of God! How unsearchable are His judgments and unfathomable His ways!... For from Him and through Him and to Him are all things" (Romans 11:33, 36 NASB). There is no reason ever to question God's actions or decisions. He does only that which is perfect in its construction, and a blessing in its action.

It is this God to whom we express our prayers. He is "closer than hands and feet; yes, than breathing itself." He knows our minds and thoughts. You may sometimes wonder, "If God is so overwhelming, why do I need to pray? He knows what I want and need without my asking." Even so, God has decreed that He responds only as we act in faith by expressing in some way or other the desires of our hearts.

<u>He is a God of LOVE.</u> Love is the essence of His being. That truth is summed up in John 3:16 – *"For God so loved the world, that He gave His only begotten Son ..."* His love is not only offered to all mankind, but He gives Himself in a special relationship to those of us who know Him in Christ, and He wants to help His children in any way they need. John records Jesus as saying, *"... for the Father Himself loves you, because you have loved Me, and have believed that I came forth from the Father."* (16:27 NASB). Jesus also said, *"If anyone loves Me, he will keep My word, and My Father will love him. ..."* (John 14:23 NASB).

There are many who pray to Jesus. There surely is nothing wrong with that. Jesus said clearly, *"And whatever you ask in My Name, that will I do, that the Father may be glorified in the Son. If you ask anything in My Name, I will do it."* (John 14:13, 14 NASB). But the Bible gives us no other indication that Jesus intended for prayer to be made to Him. Teaching His disciples, His model prayer begins, "Our Father who art in Heaven ..." His prayer in John 17 begins, *"Father, the hour has come; glorify Thy Son, that the Son may glorify Thee"* (17:1 NASB). In the Garden of Gethsemane, His prayer began, "Abba, Father" (Mark 14:36). We might justify that by the fact that these prayers were by Him as a human being. And we might also say that now, as the risen, reigning Son of God, it is O. K. to pray to Him. But His teaching about prayer was, and is, that it is to be in His Name. He said, " *...if you shall ask the Father for anything, He will give it to you in My Name"* (John 16:23

NASB). He further added, *"In that day you will ask in My Name, and I do not say that I will request the Father on your behalf, for the Father Himself loves you. ..."* (John 16:26, 27 NASB). The writer of Hebrews further affirms of Christ, *"He is able to save forever those who draw near to God through Him, since He always lives to make intercession for them"* (7:25 NASB). Those are strange words if Jesus Himself is the One to whom prayer is made.

This is not something which ought to provoke argument and confrontation. Jesus is God. But what is written above is what appears to the writer to be the truth

We have a loving, all-powerful, all-wise Heavenly Father, who knows our needs before we ask, but is ready before we ask to answer our prayers. There should be no hesitancy in approaching His throne of grace and goodness, for we know He hears us when we pray in Jesus' Name.

Much more will be said about this in Chapter 14.

Section 2 – A Good Look at Prayer

There are things about prayer as a means of communication with God, and an instrument in His hands, that are important for us to know. These are not factors in the method and act of praying, but rather are elements in the atmosphere in which biblical praying best operates. They are expressed in questions which inevitability will be asked by those who sincerely and earnestly seek to make prayer the lifeblood of their spiritual lives.

7. Is My Attitude Important?
8. What Kind of Faith Do I Need?
9. Are There Rules I Must Follow?
10. What Is Intercessory Prayer?
11. Is Church Necessary?
12. Are There Any Limits?

Seven

Is My Attitude Important?

It ought to be evident to any thinking person that one's attitude toward God and toward prayer is a giant factor in prayer becoming an important and indeed life controlling part of one's existence. One's prayer life is the thermometer measuring one's spiritual temperature. One's attitude toward prayer itself is a determining factor in whether one's prayers will ever have much effect one way or another.

When Jesus began to teach His disciples using the grapevine as His example, it is very possible that He was close by such a vine – close enough to perhaps even touch it. In any case, the vine was completely familiar to the disciples – vines were plentiful. Those men knew exactly what He was talking about when He distinguished between the vine and its branches. To speak of the vine as separate from its branches was easily understood – the vine was the thick body from which the branches grew, and the term included the roots. He was saying to the disciples, "I am the vine." It was well understood then, and is now, that there is no life in the branches except as provided by the 'vine'. If the branches have life, it is because they share in a living union between the vine and the branches. And the branches certainly can bear no fruit except as they receive nurture from the vine.

Jesus is telling the disciples that they can have no spiritual life except as He gives it, and they can produce no spiritual fruit except as they remain in complete union with Him. Without nourishment from the vine, the branches wither and die. He said, *"As the branch cannot bear fruit of itself, unless it abides in the vine, neither can you, unless you abide in Me. I am the vine, you are the branches. ."* (John 15:4, 5 NASB). Impotence in prayer rises out of some hindrance, or barrier that we permit to exist, or something lacking in the Christian's spiritual life. The problem is not with God. He hears our prayers and desires to answer them. There are several specific attitudes which are vital.

Conscious Union with Christ

Obviously, the first requirement for effective communication between us and God is full awareness of union with Christ. He said, *"If you abide in Me, and My words abide in you, ask whatever you wish, and it shall be done for you"* (John 15:7 NASB).

Since the branch can do nothing by itself but is, in reality, part of the vine, existing only for the purposes of the vine, and bearing fruit only as part of the vine, there must be an awareness that the only reason for its existence is to produce the fruit of the vine. The prayer-promise of John 15:7 is given to the branches – that's us. When the branches 'abide' in Christ – have no desire except to be as close to Him as possible, and do His will – and His 'word' abides in the branches (us) – the result will be fruit. His Word will be treasured, loved, kept, obeyed and absorbed into one's full being, and those prayer-promises will apply without restriction.

What does this mean for us? It means, first of all, that if we are to know answered prayer in any measure, we must be vitally connected to Christ. Paul tells us in his letter to the Colossians, *"If then you have been raised up with Christ, keep seeking the things above, where Christ is, seated at the right hand of God. Set your mind on things above, not on the things that are on earth. For you have died and your life is hidden with Christ in God"* (Col. 3:1-3 NASB).

It means, also, that His 'word' must have a dwelling place in us. We will love His 'word' and be willing to live by it. There must be a conscious personal closeness to Christ, and a conscious will for His 'word' and the whispers of the Holy Spirit to be the guideline for daily living. We will be spiritually fed and controlled by Him. The person with that attitude will ask only those things that are pleasing to Christ as our Lord. Jesus promises that those prayers will be answered.

A Humble Spirit

A second essential attitude for answered prayer is humility. Jesus told the story of the Publican who would not even lift up his eyes to heaven, but who beat his breast and prayed, "God, be merciful to me, the sinner." Publicans were perhaps the most despised persons in the Jewish life of that day. They were looked upon as traitors, and oppressors of their own people because they had sold themselves to become tax-gatherers for the Roman government, by means of which they became rich. So despised were they that a poor honest Jew would not accept charity from them. In the minds of the Jewish people, this kind of person was as far from God as one could be, and would be the least of all people to be heard in praying.

The Pharisee, on the other hand, was normally thought of as the most religious, the most righteous, and thus the person who would be the closest to God , and who, of all people, would be sure to be heard in his praying.

When Jesus said that the Publican's prayer was the one God heard and answered, He completely contradicted the normal thinking of his hearers. His purpose, however, was not merely to shock them, but to impress on them the truth that the reason for the Publican's being heard was his humility before God. This man knew better than anyone that he was unworthy to come to God. Yet the consciousness of his guilt drove him to seek the mercy and forgiveness of God. Note what he said, "*God, be merciful to me, THE sinner*" (Luke 18:13 NASB). He discerned that he was the lowest of the low in relationship to God.

Humility is an essential attitude in prayer. It is foolish to ignore the fact that God's actions are not dependent on our actions. We have no control over what God does, but are totally dependent on His grace. In the above parable, Jesus is teaching that the basic object of a sinner's prayer (and we are all sinners) must be for grace – God's measureless grace which is shaped by His righteousness and mercy. Frans Bakker says, "To pray for grace is yielding one's self to the sovereignty of God and simultaneously resting in the mercy of God"[2] Humility is essential, but it is not our humility which causes God to act. If our humility is purposeful – an act done with design – it is meaningless, or worse. Jesus warned, *"Beware of the scribes ...who ... for appearance's sake make long prayers; these will receive greater condemnation"* (Luke 20:46, 47 NASB). God will do nothing for the proud. The heart and spirit which is full of pride has no room for, and no receptivity toward, God's grace. Those who are rich in material resources may feel needs of many kinds, but it is only when one admits that God is the only source for fulfillment of a need that a prayer reaches Him.

The truly humble person will be keenly conscious, first of unworthiness, but also of complete dependence on God's grace. The deep desire of the heart, and the requests made in prayer, will be for the greatest of God's gifts – the spiritual blessings He offers in forgiveness, peace, wisdom, and the guidance of the Holy Spirit. These are the blessings God 'waits' to give, though He stands ready always.

All of us must come to the Father as the Prodigal Son came – in complete helplessness. . He left home with pride and arrogance, completely confident of his ability to get all there is out of life. He returned in complete humility. That humility was not generated in the conscious presence of the Father; it developed in the loneliness of a sin-conscious soul to whom none ministered. *"and no one was giving anything to him"*(Luke 15:16). In the last moments of his pride and selfishness, he was completely alone – nobody offered anything to him. *"But when he came to his senses"* – soundness of mind – he came to the Father saying, *"Father, I have sinned against heaven and in your sight; I am no longer worthy to be called your son"* (Luke 15:118. 19 NASB). In his own mind he had anticipated confessing to his father with the plea, *"Make me as one of your hired men"* (Luke 15:18, 19 NASB). He knew he deserved nothing, and expected nothing except the privilege of working humbly for the necessities of life. His faith enabled him to

---

2   Bakker, Frans: "Praying Always" p. 49.

put his life fully in the hands of the father whom he had once despised and forsaken. Now he asked only for the grace of his father. He could never repay his father the debt he owed. It was only through the grace of the father that he was now privileged to be where he was – in the presence of his father. This is the beginning point of prayer for all of us.

Boldness In Praying

A third attitude valuable in prayer is what may seem to be just the opposite of, and in contradiction to, what we have just been saying. This is the attitude of boldness in praying. There is, however, no contradiction between this kind of boldness and the needed humility. The writer of Hebrews says, *"Let us therefore come boldly to the throne of grace, that we may obtain mercy and find grace to help in time of need"* (Heb. 4:16 NKJV). Humility is the result of our seeing ourselves as we are, while boldness in prayer is a part of faith, and comes to those who know Christ for who He is, and know Him personally. This boldness is not self-assertive pride, the result of one's own preparation and strength. Rather, it is an eager willingness which grows out of trust and surrender.

The author of Hebrews knew well that this boldness is not to be found with a sinner. He points to the ground of this boldness with the word, "therefore." The basis of this is Christ who is revealed as the great high priest who has offered Himself as the sacrifice in our behalf, and who pleads our case before the Father. The Jewish high priest once a year entered the holy of holies in the temple to sprinkle the blood of sacrifice in behalf of all the people, and to ask forgiveness of their sins, including his own. That is no longer necessary, for Christ has become the interceding High Priest who is Himself the sacrifice, having paid the penalty for all our sins with His own blood. He is the Atonement for sin so that the sinner may go free. By the grace of God made visible and effective in Christ we may come boldly to the throne of grace. Nowhere does God indicate that He is ever tired of our coming, or resentful of our daring to seek His attention. On the contrary, His word to us is "Ask … seek … knock …" And His assurance given through Christ is *"the one who comes to Me, I will certainly not cast out"* (John 6:37 NASB).

Eagerness and boldness in seeking God in prayer is not a sign of arrogance or self-esteem. True boldness in Christ produces genuine humility before God. The boldness in prayer of which Hebrews speaks will always exalt and glorify the Lord Jesus. In itself it is evidence there is no dependence on human resources, but reliance only on Christ. True boldness is not generated by a sense of self-worth, but rather is the result of an awareness of helplessness bolstered by a firm faith in the grace of a loving Heavenly Father. Jesus said, *" ... unless you ... become like children, you shall not enter into the kingdom of Heaven"* (Matt. 18:3 NASB). Little children can do very little for themselves; they must be helped constantly and in so many ways. Spiritually, we must become like little children asking and receiving help. A child who knows the love of a parent does not hesitate to ask for help, but rather is bold in letting needs be known. In the same manner, we, too, can be bold.

Our boldness grows out of three things (1) Our great need; (2) Our faith that we have an Advocate with the Father; (3) The assurance that God hears and answers our prayers when we meet His requirements.

1) Our need is overwhelming. We may have far more than necessary of material resources, but it is a different picture when we assess our spiritual resources. Our weaknesses and poverty are self-evident, for our guilt and unworthiness before God cannot be denied. We are needy creatures, and like the Prodigal, we quickly learn there is no one in the secular world who can give us anything we need. Like the Prodigal we are forced to say, "But I am dying here with hunger!" (Luke 15:17cNASB).

2) When the Prodigal had exhausted all his resources, and turned to the natural world around him, he quickly found there was no one who would help him. But in his moment of greatest need, he knew where help could be found. His faith became his roadmap. He knew what sort of person his father was. He might have said, "Home is the last place I would dare go; my Father has too much against me." But he knew his father. In all of his folly he was

smart enough to remember home. Though he had sinned heinously against his father, he knew him well enough to have the faith that if he would humble himself and go home, help would be given him.

When we have heard the Word, and see ourselves as we are, poor, miserable, helpless and hopeless where we are, we then can have faith that we have an Advocate with the Father, even Jesus Christ. As the writer of Hebrews declares, *"Since then we have a great high priest who has passed through the heavens, Jesus, the Son of God, let us hold fast our confession"* (Heb. 4:14 NASB). We have nowhere else to turn for help, but we know we need no other – Jesus Christ is all we need. Like the Prodigal, we can boldly say, "I will arise and go to my Father …"(Luke 15:18a NKJV).

3) Through His Word, God gives us the assurance that He will hear our prayers. We have faith that we are loved, and we know well that *"perfect love casts out fear"* (I John 4:18). His word to us is *"the one who comes to Me I will certainly not cast out"* (John 6:37 NASB). So we are not afraid to come to Him. Though we must come to Him in the raggedness and filth of our sin, our faith enables us to approach Him with boldness knowing that we will receive mercy and *"find grace to help in time of need"* (Heb. 4:16 NASB). When we have confessed our sin and received forgiveness, and know that we are IN Christ, we have no hesitancy in bringing our petitions to the Father, knowing that our wonderful Lord intercedes for us. Boldness comes naturally.

Thankfulness of Heart

One other attitude is important – a "thankfulness of heart." This is an attitude a child of God ought to have even before a prayer is lifted up. Paul urged his readers, *"Rejoice always; pray without ceasing; in everything give thanks; for this is God's will for you in Christ Jesus"* (I Thess. 5:16-18 NASB). It is sad to admit that much of what is called 'thanksgiving' in modern prayer is mere formality, not reality. Words can be beautiful yet empty. To use the words which are meant to express a feeling of thanksgiving without the genuine spirit of gratitude is hypocrisy of the first order. There is no excuse for ingratitude; there are so many reasons why everyone of us ought to have a genuine attitude of thanksgiving. God has done so much for everyone of us. The air we breathe, the water we drink,, the food we eat, and a thousand other things are all His gifts. He is able to withhold them from us at any time if He so desires. But by His grace, He continually provides all these to both the just and the unjust without measure. Paul reminded the philosophers in Athens of this, *"The God who made the world and all things in it ... gives to all life and breath and all things ... for in Him we live and move and exist ..."* (Acts 17:24, 25, 28 NASB). Most of what we receive from God's hands we did not request. It is truly sad that so many never stop to thank Him.

Paul says it is the will of God that we thank Him in everything. Our thankfulness should never depend on fortuitous circumstances, nor even for numerous answered prayers. Our hearts should be full of gratitude that we have a God who loves us and who hears us when we cry to Him. That gratitude begins with the recognition of our weakness, helplessness, and deep need. It grows as we begin to count the many blessings we have received, and continue to receive from his bountiful hands. It reaches its crescendo as we contemplate His love toward us in Christ. It is an attitude which knows no negative situation. The true child of God will find cause for thanksgiving even in the midst of adversity. Paul and Silas sang praises to God in the midst of the night while they were probably as uncomfortable as one might be – fastened as they were in stocks in prison. (Cf. Acts 16:25). If we have an attitude of gratitude and thanksgiving which is not dependent on circumstances, then our hearts can praise Him no matter where we are, or in whatever situation we find ourselves.

The ability to be always thankful is found "in Christ Jesus." He is the gift of God; everything else is a bonus. Even as He faced the cross He could say "Father, I thank you." If we are in Christ we can do the same. The right attitude is of paramount importance for an effective prayer life. David prayed, *"Create in me a clean heart, O God, and renew a steadfast spirit within me"* (Psalm 51:10 NASB). He was asking that his attitude might be one that could be maintained always as right before God. We should ask the same.

Eight

What Kind of Faith Do I Need?

THE WRITER OF HEBREWS says, *"And without faith it is impossible to please Him, for he who comes to God must believe that He is, and that He is a rewarder of those who seek Him"* (11:6 NASB).

When Jesus and his three close disciples – Peter, James and John – came down from the Mount of Transfiguration, they found the other disciples facing a failure – they could not cure the epileptic boy. After Jesus had responded to the plea of the father and had cast out the demon which possessed the boy, the disciples asked Him, "Why could we not cast it out?", Jesus' answer was, *"Because of the littleness of your faith; for truly I say to you, if you have faith as a mustard seed, you shall say to this mountain, 'Move from here to there' and it shall move; and nothing shall be impossible to you. But this kind does not go out except by prayer and fasting"* (Matt. 17:14-21 NASB).

We have already discussed this incident from the standpoint of the reach of prayer. When one prays persistently and earnestly for a particular need, and the answer seems to be "No," there are always those who will say, "You did not have enough faith." Yet the very fact that one prays would indicate some kind of faith. Is there some special kind of faith needed? Jesus makes it plain that faith is a requirement, but just what kind of faith must it be?

God's Word says to us, *"Ask, and you shall receive. ..."* It should be obvious that a person will not ask if there is no faith in the One to whom the prayer is addressed. Why pray if you don't think there is at least the possibility of an answer? The quotation from Hebrews (above) tells us two things: First, if you are going to pray, you must believe there is a God who is real and to whom you can address your prayer; Second, you must believe that He rewards those who seek Him.

In the first verse of the Faith Chapter (Hebrews 11), the writer gives us the meaning of 'faith'. He says, *"Now faith is the assurance of things hoped for, the conviction of things not seen."*(11:1 NASB). The meaning of that is pretty clear, isn't it? It is important here to know that he is not talking about answers to prayer, but about the anticipation of eternal life. Through the entire chapter he is naming for us saints of old who trusted God all the way – in whatever circumstances they might be cast. Their faith was in God who loved them and on whom they could depend for the final ending. Their prayers for immediate help were not always granted. But they did not lose faith in God. They acted on the basis that they were willing to trust God for the outcome. The writer says, *"All these died in faith, without receiving the promises, but having seen them and having welcomed them from a distance..."*(11:13 NASB),

Paul gives us the same lesson. He prayed for his "thorn in the flesh" to be removed. The answer was always "No." But that was not the final answer. God added, *"My grace is sufficient for you, for power is perfected in weakness."* (Cf .2 Cor. 12:7-9).

Jesus, in the Garden of Gethsemane, prayed *"My Father, if it is possible, let this cup pass from Me"* (Matt. 26:29 NASB). Jesus did not waste words. This was not a stage dressing. It is the prayer of a human being facing an awful possibility. But His humanity demanded that He express His awareness of what He knew He would endure, and thus asking God "Is there any other way"? No one, not even Jesus Christ, would delight in the suffering He knew lay before Him. His faith in the Father was so complete that He trusted God for what ever might come.

Was it that Paul and Jesus did not have enough faith? Stupid question. It was not lack of faith on their part. Rather it was their faith which enabled them to move through what they faced.

Does this mean that the writer of Hebrews was wrong? No, indeed! What it means is that we must realize that the writer is talking about faith in far larger terms that just hoping and believing God will give me what I ask for. We must recognize that 'faith' has several definitions in the Scriptures, all of which have a bearing on the matter of prayer.

The first and most important lesson for us to learn is that biblical 'faith' is not 'faith in faith.' It is not believing something will become reality because we believe it will be. There is a rash of false teaching which says, "If you believe hard enough, it will be so." That is not so. God will not be manipulated by our determination, nor by our apparent need. We will not force Him to do what we want by the power of our so-called 'faith.'

True faith is complete trust. It is putting one's self completely in God's hands, willing to trust Him for whatever He does, or doesn't do. In the Garden, Jesus added, *"My Father, if this cannot pass away unless I drink it, Thy will be done."* (Matt. 26:42 NASB). He had been sent for a specific purpose (Cf. John 4:34; 8:29). His faith was such that He was willing to trust the Father in all that He was called to do, including the cross. Such faith rests upon the assurance that God loves us, and that, because of His love, He will do for us what He knows is best for us, but above and beyond that, God's priority is the Kingdom of God. How do you fit in that plan? He wants to bless you, but the greatest blessing He can bestow on you is to see to it that you fit in the greater plan for His Kingdom. If you are a child of God, He will never ignore your prayer. His answer to a prayer may be a flat "No.!" It also may be, "Not now." And it also may be, "I have something better than that for you." But we can be sure that He hears and will answer in His own wise way in His own good time.

Life is a pilgrimage; it never stands still; there is constant movement. The present is but a moment which is gone as soon as a person is aware of it. Any kind of faith must, of necessity, look to the future and believe in something beyond this moment. All prayer, except thanksgiving, is posited to the future. It must be based on one's confidence that God not only can do what is asked, but that He wants to give His blessings and good things to His children. In that sense, prayer is always looking forward with expectancy.

It is so important, however, to be mindful that *"God is Spirit, and those who worship Him must worship in spirit and truth"* (John 4:24 NASB). Those who are on speaking terms with God know that the most important aspects of life cannot be seen with the physical eye -- they are "things not seen." Consequently, the person of faith looks beyond the apparent circumstances and seeks to discern the presence and activity of God in every event or situation. The basis of this faith is the Word of God. We do not grasp such concepts out of thin air. If God did not reveal Himself to us through His Word, written and living, we would know nothing about Him, or about His love and His grace. But He has revealed His purpose and His plan, His love and His mercy, through the Living Word who is Jesus Christ, and it is given to us in the testimony of the written Word, the Bible, which is the source of our information. It is impossible to know God apart from His Word. And it is impossible to have an intelligent faith in Him unless we know Him in Person.

The writer of Hebrews also tells us that God gives His approval to those who exercise the right kind of faith. He says *"For by it the men of old received divine approval"* (Heb. 11:2 RSV). This approval is not a mere passive acceptance; rather, it is a warm and positive commendation; in fact, it is the witness of God. The person who lives by faith in God knows that his or her life has divine approbation. That does not mean God approves of everything we do. But it does mean God accepts our faith, which He has given to us, as the mark of our relationship to Him. As Ronald Dunn has put it, "Everything God demands of man can be summed up in one word: faith." The writer of Hebrews declares "And without faith it is impossible to please Him" (11:6a NASB).

What Kind of Faith Do I Need? 77

Faith is essential in prayer because it is the only means by which we can become aware of the power of God. Unbelief denies that God can do anything outside the normal sphere of human rationality and understanding. The writer of Hebrews says, *"By faith we understand that the worlds were prepared(put in shape) by the word of God, so that what is seen was not made out of things which are visible"* (11:3 NASB). God's creation is not merely a transformation of one material into another form. He made all that is seen out of nothing. And He did it by simply saying the word. The Bible tells us, *"Then God said, 'Let there be light' and there was light."* (Gen. 1:3 NASB). Faith is believing in that kind of God. The angel, speaking to Mary, put it in words for us, *"For nothing will be impossible with God"* (Luke 1:37 NASB). When faith lays hold of that truth, there is no question as to God's power to do anything He wants to do.

Belief in the existence of God is irrelevant unless accompanied by a commitment to Him as the most important fact in life. Without that commitment life ultimately becomes meaningless. If you have real faith in God, you will want to come closer to Him. He will be the desire of your life. Not only that, but you will have no doubt that He is, indeed, the rewarder of all those who seek Him.

We do not hunger for God and remain empty. Nothing in this life is more rewarding than to seek consciously to enter into His presence. Those who consciously live in His presence can testify to His reality and His goodness.

Dr. F. B. Meyer, in his book, "The Way Into the Holiest" says there are three necessary preliminaries if faith is to be real: (1) Someone must make a promise; (2) There must be a good reason to believe in the integrity, and the ability, of the one who makes the promise; (3) There follows the assurance that the promise is as good as kept before it happens.

Those three conditions are fulfilled in the Christian faith. (1) We are sure a voice has spoken to us from the pages of Holy Scripture, with a promise. In John 17:8 Jesus said, in His prayer, *"For I gave them the words you gave Me, and they accepted them."* (NIV). (2) We are sure this voice is credible. In the same verse Jesus also says, *"They knew with certainty that I came from You, and they believed that You sent Me"*. (3) Because of all that Jesus said and did, and because of the work of the promised Holy Spirit, we know that what has been promised is a reality – we can depend on it.

Faith is the ground on which all prayer stands. There is no prayer without faith of some kind. And faith always implies another – some entity beyond one's self. The Christian is fully supplied with One in Whom to have faith. He has promised to hear us and answer. We believe fully in His reality, and in His integrity. We also believe He has all power, and nothing is impossible with Him. He is not a figment of our imagination. He has sent His only begotten Son to be His Word to us, and all that He has done is given to us in His written Word on which we can count with the same confidence and assurance as that which we have in Him. In addition, as we pray in faith, we can experience a growing awareness of His activity within our own lives.

There are several things we must remember in this matter of 'faith' as it relates to prayer:

First, <u>God wills only good.</u> He never wills evil. His desire and will for all mankind is only good. It is obvious, then, that His purpose and plans for those who are His children by faith can be and is only what is good. We do not have to wonder and worry if God will ever cause anything bad to happen to us. Love will never hurt, unless good can come from it. His Word says, *"And we know God causes all things to work together for good to those who love God, to those who are called according to His purpose"* (Romans 8:28 NASB). This is a sinful world, full of evil. Even though we are children of God, we cannot escape the evil activities of this world. But if we trust God, we know that He will be at work in 'all things' to bring good to us. All that He does is good, for it comes from One who is 'Love.'

Second, <u>faith enables us to base all of life – our actions and attitudes – on the conviction that truth is eternal, and is the foundation stone for all of life.</u> Jesus declared, *". . you shall know <u>the truth</u>, and the truth shall make you free"* (John 8:32 NASB). He also said, *"I am the way, <u>the truth</u>, and the life: no one comes to the Father but through Me"* (John 14:6 NASB). Jesus is the focal point of our faith. The Word declares, *"He* *who believes in the Son has eternal life; but he who does not obey the Son shall not see life, but the wrath of God abides on him"* (John 3:36 NASB). When we pray, it is because of our faith in Jesus Christ. We not only pray in His Name, but it is because of His teaching and example that we have faith enough to approach God in prayer. The prayer of all who are outside of Christ is but a cry into empty darkness except when that cry is a call for help for a sinful life- "God be merciful to me, the sinner."

Third, Jesus also taught His disciples that <u>faith is not only the basis for prayer, but it must be the motivation and the dynamics of prayer.</u> On both of the occasions when Jesus went back to His home town, Nazareth, He was unable to do much for those people because they did not believe in Him. On one occasion two blind men followed Him crying out to Him, "Have mercy on us, son of David." When they came up to Him, He said to them, *"Do you believe that I am able to do this?"* Their reply was "Yes, Lord." His answer then was to touch their eyes and say, *"Be it done unto you according to your faith."* (Cf. Matt. 9:27-29).

Fourth, <u>faith is not just believing in facts, it is primarily trust.</u> We have previously quoted from Hebrews, *"…he who comes to God must believe that He is, and that He is a rewarder of those who seek Him"* (11:6 NASB). That means we never come to God without receiving His blessings. Experience quickly tells us that we do not always receive what our finite and sinful minds may decide we need or want. What is promised are the blessings God wants to give us. **Real faith in God, then, is to trust Him fully.** It is to say with Job, *"Though He slay me, yet will I trust Him …"* (11:15 NKJV). If we truly trust Him, we will leave the answer to Him, and be grateful for what He does, saying as did our Lord, *"Not my will, but Thine be done"* (Luke 22:42).

Fifth, <u>we must be careful we do not replace 'faith in God' with 'faith in faith'.</u> It is easy for someone to say "All you need to do is have enough faith and your prayers will be answered." It is important, however, to remember two things: (1) Jesus' words about faith and prayer included the restriction "in My Name" (Cf. John 14:13, 14 – see Chapter 13). (2) The faith required is 'faith in God' not 'faith in faith.'

It is imperative to remember that the faith Jesus honors is not believing your prayer will be answered simply because you believe it will be. Faith in faith says, ""My faith is such that God has to do what I want done." With that attitude, 'faith' becomes the 'god' we depend upon, which really means faith in ourselves. 'Faith in God' is not an instrument we can use to get what we want. Real faith in God is to want what He wants.

Sixth., it is <u>important not to misunderstand and misuse those wonderful statements of Jesus concerning prayer.</u> Jesus said, " ... *that whatever you ask of the Father in My name, He may give it to you*" (John 15:16 NASB). He also said, "*And whatever you ask in My name, that will I do, that the Father may be glorified in the Son. If you ask anything in My name, I will do it*" (John 14:13-14 NASB). There are other verses of a similar nature. The question we must ask as we try to claim the promises in those verses is, "Is Jesus giving to all who believe in Him a blank check signed in His Name?" The answer is "Yes – if we are asking for those things which are in the will of God; No – if we are praying for those things which are selfish, or foolish, or what is not in God's will." Jesus' preface to all our praying is "*Seek first His Kingdom and His righteousness; and all these things shall be added to you*" (Matt. 6:33 NASB).

We cannot escape the conclusion that Jesus is telling us our priority at all times is to be the Kingdom and the righteousness of God. As long as those are the parameters of our praying, whatever we ask in His Name will be given gladly, generously, but always with the guidance of God's foreknowledge and wisdom. Many times God does not give what we ask even when it seems to us to be the very thing He would want us to have. His reason is that His timing is always better than ours. When the time is right, in His planning, He will act. His wisdom is far greater than ours, and there are times when He does not give what we ask in order to give us something better. He waits until we are wise enough, and Spirit-led, so we will grow spiritually to the place that we will ask something better. It is important that our 'faith' be the right kind. Always we can pray, "Lord, I believe; help my unbelief."

Nine

What Are the Rules?

WHEN THE CONCEPT OF 'rules for praying' is brought into the picture many folk will think in terms of physical posture, physical action, or required location and circumstances. The Bible tells us of a number of different situations in which prayer took place – the Pharisee and the Publican prayed on the street corner; Hannah prayed in the tabernacle at Shiloh; Jesus prayed on the mountain side; Paul prayed on the highway; Mary prayed in the seclusion of her home; Paul and Silas prayed in prison. . The place is not important. One can pray anywhere, and in almost any circumstance. You can pray in church; you can pray at home; you can pray driving down the highway. And the physical attitude or circumstance is not critical. Paul and Silas were in stocks; Elijah prayed with his face between his knees; Solomon knelt on his knees; Ezekiel fell on his face in prayer; Paul instructed "...*pray, lifting up holy hands, without wrath or dissension*" (I Tim. 2:8 NASB).

Commonsense tells us that we ought to pray in an atmosphere and in a position which helps us to express our reverence in the sight of God, and in such an attitude and position as will enable us to keep our minds on what we are doing. The important thing is to pray – communicate with God in praise, thanksgiving, petition.

We can assume that every thinking person has his or her own ideas about prayer. But perhaps we can also assume that anyone who has any idea at all about prayer will realize that the Bible teaches very clearly there are, in a sense, some rules to follow. They are simple and clear. Prayer is not tied up in a complicated formula which must be followed. Every true born-again believer in Jesus Christ has access to God in prayer. Yet there are a few basic principles which the Scripture lays out for us.

At the outset, it should be obvious that for prayer to be heard by God, it must be real prayer – not just saying a few words in a formula called 'prayer'. The words chosen, and the form followed, are not important. Prayer can be a groan, a cry, a hand outreached, as well as perfectly formed phrases. Real prayer is an effort to communicate with God about a person's needs or deep-seated desires, or express praise and thanksgiving, or whatever else one would want to talk about to God. The writer of Hebrews tells us, "... *he who comes to God must believe that He is, and that He is a rewarder of those who seek Him."* (11:6 NASB). Real prayer is the earnest effort to communicate with God about the things that are important to you. He cannot be seen, but He is there, and He listens.

First, let's be sure we are clear as to what prayer is not –

1. It is not just the voicing of a request – that may be speaking to the wind – throwing out a plea for help without any real awareness of the Person to whom it is addressed. The atheist sliding down a housetop may cry out "O my God – ". That may not be any more prayer than fingering prayer beads. Prayer is the earnest effort of the suppliant to communicate with the Supplier.

2. It is not just repeating 'prayer' words – vain repetitions, as the Bible puts it. We are not heard for our much speaking, even if we say what we think are the right words. Prayer, at times, may be the groping outreach of blindness, but it is more than just the flailing of words with the hope somebody out there will

hear. Prayer is the utterance of the heart towards One whom faith says is there and listening.

3. Real prayer is not informing God of what we think He ought to know. A seminary student who did mission work in a city downtown area, in a prayer said, "God, you would be surprised at what we find down there." Jesus told His disciples that God knows our needs before we ask. We don't have to explain to Him what our need is.

4. Prayer does not require beautiful words and an unctuous tone. God is not necessarily turned off by beautiful words. But the choice of words and tone of voice guarantee nothing. God pays attention only to the genuineness of the plea.

5. Prayer is not using the voice to perform an act to be seen and heard by others. Hypocrisy in any form eradicates prayer. Jesus said, *"And when you pray you shall not be as the hypocrites are ..."*(Matt. 6:5) This is always a danger for those who pray in public.

Jesus gave us some guidelines for praying, and there are other bits of Instruction in the Scripture.

First, prayer should be a habit, a custom, a pattern of life. It was so with Jesus Himself. Luke says of Him, *"Now He was telling them a parable to show that at all times they ought to pray and not lose heart"* (Luke 18:1 NASB). Paul tells us, *"Rejoice always, pray without ceasing, in everything give thanks; for this is the will of God in Christ Jesus for you"* (1 Thess. 5:16-18 NKJV). Prayer is to be a way of life. Before Jesus gave to the disciples the Model Prayer, He said to them, *"When you pray ..."* He expected His disciples to pray, and He set the example for them, to make prayer a vital part of life. The Model Prayer indicates that it is to be an every day occurrence, *"Give us this day. . "*

Second, prayer is to be a purely personal, even secret, activity, most of the time. There obviously will be times when it is not only proper, but desirable, that prayer be public. But most of the time an individual's praying will be when there is no one there but that person and God. Jesus said, *"Shut thy door ..."* He prayed out of doors much more often than He did indoors, it appears, so He did not mean we should pray only when we have gone into an inner closet. He was saying we should shut the doors of our minds and consciousness to the outside world, and close ourselves in with God. In the secret of our own hearts we will shut out everyone and everything else in order to be alone with God.

For those who have difficulty focusing their attention on God, it may help to use a very simple exercise. Do as Jesus said – get off by yourself in a room where there is no other human being. Concentrate attention on God. If there is difficulty in keeping attention focused on Him, put a chair opposite and ask God to occupy that chair. Let your prayer – whether thanksgiving, praise or petition – be directed to your God whom you have asked to be in the vicinity of that chair. – A church member was the victim of a lengthy illness. The pastor visited him regularly. One day the pastor asked the sick man's daughter if there was any particular significance in a chair which had been against a wall but lately would sit close by the bed. She did not know, but assured the pastor she would find out. When she asked her father why the chair was constantly close to his bed, he told her "The Lord Jesus sits there." On the next visit, the pastor asked the man about it. In reply the sick man said, "I was having trouble praying. God did not seem to be close. But the speaker on a radio program had said, "If you have trouble praying because God seems to be way off yonder, just put a chair close to you and ask the Lord to sit there as you pray. So I did that, and He is always there."

Prayer is a personal transaction between the individual and God. Only those who shut themselves in with God can really pray. Wherever we are, we are to "shut the door," so as to be undisturbed by the world. Even in the midst of milling crowds, roaring machinery, and bewildering perplexities there can be a secret place where you and God can fellowship.

Jesus is also saying that we are take down any signs that we may be praying. Prayer is not a ceremony. Jesus said, *"And when you pray, you are not to be as the hypocrites; for they love to stand and pray in the synagogues and on street corners, in order to be seen by men"* (Matt. 6:5 NASB).

He is saying: Don't call attention it; don't try to appear religious. It is a personal vis-a-vis with God.

Third, we are to pray definitely and specifically. On one occasion, as Jesus was coming out of Jericho, two blind men, learning that Jesus was passing by, cried out to Him, "Lord, have mercy on us, Son of David." When Jesus spoke to them, His question was, *"What do you want Me to do for you?"* (Matt. 20:30, 32 NASB). He wanted them to express exactly what their needs were, and what they believed He could do for them. Paul tells us, " *...in everything by prayer and supplication with thanksgiving let your requests be made known unto God"*(Phil. 4:6 NASB). It seems evident that God wants us to be specific in what we ask, not to inform Him, but to direct our prayers that they may be in faith. A dear woman said, 'When you pray for me, don't bunch me." She wanted to be prayed for in her own name, not just as part of an unnamed group.

Just here we face a problem – praying for our missionaries. There are thousands of them all of whom have needs, many of those urgent. But it is impossible to know all their names, and if we did, time would limit the ones we could cover in prayer. But it is so much better to pray for a few by name. Obviously, we want God to bless all of them, and we ought to pray to that end. But when we pray for them as a group, we have no idea of their personal, specific needs. How much better it is to make the effort to learn the names of a few, and then seek to know their specific needs so that we can truly ask God to provide their real needs.

God knows our needs before we ask. But He definitely wants us to be specific in our praying. He gets no joy out of our laziness, inattention, or muddled thinking. All that God does is logical, and He wants us to have the same pattern. Know what you really need, and even what you want; then don't waste time. Communicate your needs to God as you would to your best friend sitting right in front of you. Tell Him in the fewest words possible what your request is.

Fourth, we are to pray <u>submissively.</u> That does not mean to pray with quaking fear, but it does mean to pray with reverence. And it means being willing to wait on God to answer you in His own good way and His own good time. He may keep us waiting for a while; and He may say "No" to a specific request. But if we have true faith in Him, we will be willing to trust His love, His wisdom, and His judgment. Submissive prayer is being willing to make our wills fully cooperative with His eternal will. Perhaps each time we make a request of God, we ought to ask – Why should God grant this request? Is it purely personal and only for my own pleasure and selfish benefit, or is it something for which God may have some concern?

Fifth, we are to pray <u>persistently</u>. That does not mean we will lay siege to heaven's doors until somebody responds. It does mean we will continue to ask in faith believing God will hear and answer us if what we ask is worthy of His consideration. If the Holy Spirit does not make us aware that what we ask for is outside the will of God, then our faith will enable us to persist – it is an expression of our trust in the love, wisdom and mercy of God. If we are led by the Spirit, He will help us know if what we are asking is unworthy, or contrary to the Father's will.

George Mueller is said to have prayed for the salvation of two of his friends for more than fifty years. One of them was saved shortly before Mr. Mueller died, and the other within a few months after his death. Our Lord encouraged persistence in prayer.

Sixth, prayer should always include a time of praise for God. Jesus began the Model Prayer with the words, *"Our Father, who art in heaven, hallowed be Thy Name ..."* When Jesus was asked, "Teacher, which is the great commandment in the law?" His reply was, *"You shall love the Lord your God with all your heart, and with all your soul,. And with all your mind."* (Matt. 22: 36, 37 NASB). In the Model prayer, He gave priority to the glorification of the Name of God. We live in a time when there seems to be little respect, or reverence, for anything. God's Name is taken in vain by so many, and is so carelessly used even by so-called Christians. Using the Model Prayer, we approach God as a Person, not just an automatic teller machine that will grant our request if we have the proper card and code number. God is *"Our Father, who art in heaven."* We are to approach Him with utmost reverence. He is not merely "the Man upstairs." One of the greatest problems today is that we have lost the sense of wonder at the marvels of God – not His power and miracles – but God Himself. There are so few who appear to stand in awe of our God who is high and holy. Holiness is a word diminished in its meaning by a secular, familiarizing world. The surest way to human and earthly decay , ordinariness and destruction is to profane the Name of God. Wherever God's Name is held in high honor, there you will find man at his best. We are carefully instructed to lift that wonderful Name high.

Seventh, Jesus instructed that the second petition, and in a sense the one which should have priority in our lives and prayers, is to be *"Thy kingdom come, Thy will be done on earth as it is in heaven."* The average person has the idea that the purpose of prayer is to ask for the personal blessings we need, or desire. But here Jesus is saying that the basic purpose of prayer is to seek the completion of God's plan for His Kingdom, and that includes the accomplishment of His will here on earth. We live in a world fatally marred by sin. Satan, called in the Bible "the god of this age", has large control over the actions of a large majority of the population. We have every right to be distressed by what we see manifested almost everywhere. If, like Lot, our souls *"are tormented day after day by their lawless deeds"* (Cf. II Peter 2:8) we will long for justice, righteousness and peace, and our hearts will cry out with this prayer *"Thy kingdom come. Thy will be done on earth as it is in heaven."*

Jesus makes it quite plain that His preface to all our praying is *"Seek first His kingdom and His righteousness. ."* (Matt. 6:33 NASB). We cannot escape the conclusion that He is telling us our priority at all times is to be the Kingdom and righteousness of God. God wants our priority in life to be the same as His. He wants us to come to the place that what we want in life more than anything else is that God's rule on this earth and in this world will be total – He will be King of kings over all creation. We will yearn and constantly pray for His righteousness to be the standard for all mankind. We will seek with all our energies to help the Kingdom of God to be a reality everywhere. We will work and pray that God's will – His desire and purposes – will be dominant everywhere. Nothing should supersede that in our lives.

We will hunger to see the will of God effective in all civilization – in government, in business, in the homes, in recreation, in all society, as well as in the church.

Consequently, it is important to be fully aware what we are saying when we pray this prayer, *"Thy will be done on earth as it is in heaven."* Have you thought seriously about it? If you mean what you are saying, you are asking God's will to be done in your own life first. It is hypocritical in the extreme to pray for God's will to be done in other lives if the one praying is not willing for that to be true in his or her own life. But once we have crossed that hurdle, having taken care of our own little world in its proper orientation, then we have every right to pray that God's will may be the guiding, constraining, enabling force which shapes the world around us.

Eighth, Jesus taught that three other personal petitions should be included in our praying. They focus on the three greatest perennial needs of those who are Kingdom subjects – needs with which all of us are familiar: bread – food; forgiveness – personal relationships; and victory – in our personal lives and in the spiritual world of which we are a part.

We are to pray for these personal needs – but there are specifics we are to note. We are to pray for our food, *"Give us this day our daily bread"* – for today, not tomorrow. If we could build up a storehouse full of what we will need, then we likely would do just as the foolish man who said, "I don't have room to store all I have, so I will build bigger barns, then I will be able to say, "Soul, take your ease.""

In the world of Jesus' day, this prayer was sharply applicable. It was an agrarian society, in a poverty level economy. Many things could affect the food supply. For many people, food was on a day-to-day order. There was no way to preserve food other than grain, and that was subject to disappearance in many ways. The humble child of God knew full well that God provided all the food there was, and it was subject to seasons, weather, disasters. Jesus wanted His disciples to be fully aware of where their security was. It was not in themselves or in their barns, but in God who sent the rain and sun, and caused the seed to sprout, grow and produce.

In our largely urban society, it may be more difficult for some to be keenly aware of God's part in providing for our needs. But the implication of the prayer is the same. God wants us to be fully aware that we are dependent on Him to provide for us wherever we are. It is so easy to take for granted our ease of life – the stores are full. But we need to recognize how easy it would be for God to upset our complicated supply system. Katrina and the Gulf Coast disaster should be a reminder. If the trains and trucks were to stop running for two weeks, millions of Americans would go hungry, even if money was plentiful.

The Christian gratefully acknowledges that God gives us all things that are essential to life. Even with food stored in the pantry, refrigerator and freezer, there is no guarantee it will be available tomorrow. When hurricanes blow through, the area often is left with no electricity, no gas for cooking, and perhaps even no safe water. We are dependent on God, and we ought to acknowledge it to Him every day.

The second of these personal petitions is *"Forgive us our trespasses as we forgive those who trespass against us."* The accomplishment of God's will in this earthly portion of His Kingdom depends to a large extent on relationships – our relationship with God and our relationships with people, particularly other Christians. Forgiveness is our great need before God, and willingness to forgive is the critical factor determining our relationships with our fellowmen. If we want fellowship with God, then we must have His forgiveness. Unconfessed, unforgiven sin is a solid barrier separating us from God so far as fellowship is concerned. If we want fellowship with God, then we must have His forgiveness, and that is not available except as we are right with our fellowmen. We can't have one without the other.

Jesus made it quite plain, *"But if you do not forgive men, then your Father will not forgive your transgressions."* It is the love of God which enables Him to forgive us our sins and transgressions. And it is God's love in us which enables us to do the same toward those who sin against us. Where there is a lack of love there is usually an unforgiving spirit. And such a spirit effectively destroys all possibility of God achieving

His purposes. Those who have an unforgiving spirit have no access to God in prayer until the willingness to forgive has been retrieved.

This prayer is an acknowledgment of our human sinfulness and our need to have access to God. It is also acknowledgment that we know full well God will not forgive us our sins until, and unless, we are willing to let His spirit of love and forgiveness work toward others.

The third petition is *"Lead us not into temptation, but deliver us from evil, for Thine is the Kingdom, the power and the glory."* Do you desire to lead a life that will exalt Christ, and bring honor and glory to God? If so, then this prayer is essential. We live in such a sinful, wicked world, and temptations are constantly being thrust upon us. If we are to live a life pleasing to Christ then we will need to pray this prayer often. Jesus is not saying that God will, in any sense, or way, lead us into temptation – far from it. James is firm in telling us, *"Let no one say when he is tempted, 'I am tempted by God'; for God cannot be tempted by evil; nor does He Himself tempt anyone"* (James 1:13 NKJV). Not only is it true that God does not tempt us; He uses all His wisdom and power to help us turn our backs on temptation. If we are obedient children, we will be led by the Holy Spirit in all we do. This prayer, then, is asking that God will, by His Spirit, lead us in such a way that we will not be faced with temptation, but will, instead, be delivered from evil.

We must recognize and admit that God permits us to be tempted. He permitted His Son, Jesus Christ, to be tempted, even as we are, in all points. His humanity would always be questioned if it were not affirmed that He was *"tempted in all things as we are, yet without sin"* (Heb. 4:15 NASB). There are two things that are important to remember when we think about this:(1) These were real temptations. Some argue that Jesus, being the Son of God, COULD NOT SIN. If that is true, then the Bible lies, for it says He was tempted just as we are. The account of these temptations is not just window-dressing. Jesus WAS tempted. (2) His standing firm against temptation was NOT due to His being the divine Son of God, but because in His humanity, He was strengthened by the Holy Spirit in the same way we are. He could have sinned, but DID NOT. In the same way we can stand firm against temptation. If we have committed ourselves to do the will of God, we will resolve not to sin.

If we have the mind of Christ, we will certainly desire victory over evil in our own lives. For we are part of God's Kingdom, and thus a factor in His battle against Satan and evil and unrighteousness. For a victory in our lives is a vital part in God's world victory. It is essential, then, that we pray for strength from our Lord to enable us to overcome anything that would destroy our fellowship and our witness.

This prayer ends with acclamation of the rule and power and glory of God. The true child of God will always be gratified at the thought of the wonderful day when God's Kingdom will be established in total fruition of all its pristine power and glory – when Jesus will be truly King of kings and Lord of lords in its fullness. These petitions give us a skeleton outline of the truest purposes of prayer. The lesson is clear that our requests of a personal nature are not the large function of prayer, but that God's purpose in giving us the privilege of prayer is to share with Him in the establishment of His Kingdom and rule over all His creation.

Ten

What Is Intercessory Prayer?

"INTERCESSORY" IS A BIG word, but it simply means "in behalf of somebody else." Intercessory prayer is prayer in behalf of someone other than one's self. It is lifting up a petition to the Heavenly Father in behalf of others in their need. No matter what the specific request may be, when we seek God's help for somebody else, that is "intercessory prayer."

The usual thought is that it is a person's physical needs for which we ought to pray – poor health or life threatening illness, the death of a loved one, financial needs, or other problems. But for the Christian, there are many other opportunities. This is a ministry open to all believers regardless of handicaps, problems, obstacles, opposition, or even prohibitions. There is nothing that can prevent one person praying for another except one's own unwillingness. The person who is bedfast and immobile, if mentally alert, can still pray. The person handicapped by deafness or inability to speak can still lift up earnest petitions in behalf of others. Even the person who is sternly forbidden to pray, perhaps under threat of death, cannot be prevented from lifting up a petition in the secret of his or her own soul.

Jesus is our supreme example in the ministry of "intercessory prayer." He assured Peter, even as He foretold Peter's denial, *"But I have prayed for you, that your faith should not fail."* (Luke 22:32 **NKJV**). And it did not. Though Peter denied his Lord, he came through that bitter experience with penitence and forgiveness. In Jesus' great prayer found in John 17 – 'the Lord's own prayer' – we can see the place that intercessory prayer occupied in His mind and heart. In that prayer He said, *"I ask on their behalf ... those whom Thou hast given Me ... Holy Father, keep them in Thy name ... that they may be one, even as We are ... that they may have My joy made full in themselves. .keep them from the evil one ...sanctify them in the truth ...that they also may be in Us ...that they may be perfected in unity ... Father, I desire that they also ...be with Me where I am, that they also may behold My glory which Thou hast given Me ..."* (Cf. John 17:9-24 **NASB**).

There are many beautiful examples of intercessory prayer in the Bible. The prophet Samuel, who was a wise, practical leader and judge of Israel, prayed often for his people. At the end of his life and ministry, his words were, *"Moreover, as for me, far be it from me that I should sin against the Lord by ceasing to pray for you"* (I Samuel 12:23 **NASB**). Samuel is not assuming the load of praying for everybody, but he was aware of the responsibility laid upon him with his Judgeship of his nation. God had somehow said to him, "They are yours; don't neglect them." God will lay somebody on your heart and mind, and it would be sinful for you not to pray for those so positioned. And surely there are those whom you love, and others for whom you have special regard, who have their problems, burdens and needs. Surely you will pray for them. That is intercessory prayer.

Praying for Those in Authority

In the New Testament we are instructed and urged to pray for others who are not Christians. Paul wrote to Timothy, *"I urge that entreaties and prayers, petitions and thanksgivings, be made on behalf of all men, for kings and all who are in authority"* (I Tim. 2:1, 2 **NASB**). He gave a very good reason for such prayers, *"...in order that we may lead a tranquil and quiet life in all godliness and dignity"* (2:2b **NASB**). Prayer for those in authority is of vital importance if we are to be able to lead a quiet and peaceable life. Christians ought to pray for all who are in places of authority – local, state, national, and even international. Those prayers may be selfish, for we certainly want our personal situations to be improved. But surely it is not difficult to move over to the spirit which desires that the situation – locally, nationally, internationally – may open to the way for the Kingdom of God to come nearer to its fruition.

Praying for Our Enemies

Jesus also taught that we ought to pray for our enemies. Maybe you have no personal enemies you can identify, but there are enemies of the cross of Christ all around us – atheists, agnostics, skeptics, humanists, criminals, drug lords, gamblers, the lawless at any level. It is not easy to pray for these, but easy to condemn. Jesus, however, gave us specific instructions, *"But I say to you, love your enemies and pray for those who persecute you"* (Matt. 5:44 NASB). He gave us the perfect example as they lifted Him up on the cross. His prayer for all those who had any part in His trial and crucifixion was: *"Father, forgive them, for they do not know what they are doing"* (Luke 23:34 NASB). Stephen, as he was being stoned to death, followed the example of His Lord, *"Lord, do not hold this sin against them."* (Acts 7:60 NASB).

The true Christian has no difficulty praying for those whom he or she loves. But you cannot pray for a person you hate. You may wish to call down the wrath of God on him, but you cannot ask the blessings of God on him unless you love him. Your lips may say one thing, but your heart will desire another. The best way to get rid of enemies is to turn them into friends. Even if they are not changed in their attitude toward you, when you pray for them, they become those whom you love. That kind of love is not a feeling, or an emotion. It has to be of the will, by which you bring yourself to genuinely desire good for those who hate you. That is not easy, but it is God's will for true Christians.

Praying for Those We Love

From observation, it seems obvious that much of the praying for others is for physical or material needs. We pray for the sick, those who sorrow, or have heavy burdens and great problems. Sometimes we pray for God to open the way for a friend, and smooth the road. There is nothing wrong with such prayers. We live in a material world, and many of our problems and needs are of a material nature. But Jesus has taught us that these should not be the dominant feature in our praying. The divine concept of prayer is a desire for spiritual strength and blessings.

No one questions the need or the value of prayer in behalf of others for healing and health. James tells us, *"Is anyone among you sick? Let him call for the elders of the church, and let them pray over him, anointing him with oil in the Name of the Lord, and the prayer offered in faith will restore the one who is sick, and the Lord will raise him up"* (James 5:14, 15 NASB). That raises a problem for us, in that we know of times when the whole church has prayed for a dear saint, yet healing has not taken place. In no sense would we question the Scripture. But we remember that Paul asked for healing, yet it was not granted. Our hearts tell us we ought to follow the counsel of James, but at the same time acknowledge that God does not give us control at any time. God heals infinitely more times than He denies healing. But He does not let us call the shots, so to speak. Prayers of faith have been, are and will be heard and answered. But God does not turn us loose to run the universe at any point, no matter how faithful we may be. Healing is still His specialty, and He uses it according to His perfect wisdom and knowledge. I am convinced that James, in no sense, is making a guarantee. What he is saying is a perfectly acceptable and wonderfully beneficial pattern to follow. When one is sick, we, as individuals ought to pray for that one, and certainly the church ought to lift up prayer in that person's behalf. But in every instance, the person of faith will gladly submit to the will of God, whatever that may be.

Prayer for those who are lost, without Christ, is an imperative. Jesus said. *"For the Son of Man has come to seek and to save that which was lost"* (Luke 19:10 NASB). Paul set the example for us. He declared, *"Brethren, my heart's desire and my prayer to God for them is for their salvation"* (Rom. 10:1 NASB). Peter affirmed the need saying, *"The Lord ... is patient toward you, not wishing for any to perish but for all to come to repentance*" (II Peter 3:9 NASB). It is easy to say, "Lord, save all the lost people" but there is not much value in that. A real concern for the lost will find its focal point in those whom we know are unsaved. If we really care, we quickly learn that earnest prayer for the salvation of one we know demands an agonizing soul. If we have a divine view of the terror of hell, then prayer for the salvation of those we know and love will not be the careless mouthing of a few words. It will be prayer burdened with the heaviness of anxiety.

Every Christian ought to have a prayer list, and predominant in that should be those who give no evidence of knowing Jesus Christ as Lord and Savior. Praying for these is essential. Only the Holy Spirit can convict of sin, righteousness, judgment. All our efforts to witness, persuade, convince and change will be fruitless unless the Holy Spirit uses those efforts to bring conviction. It is His power which is essential. But the wonder is that God uses our prayers, in proportion to our earnestness, to bring conviction and conversion. It is also vital that we not lose heart in praying for the lost. How long should you pray for a lost person? How long would you want someone to pray for you if you were not saved? It is God's will that none shall perish, and that being true, then as long as there is life there is hope.

Praying for Fellow Christians

Paul sets the example for us. In eleven of his thirteen letters he writes asking for prayer for himself and his ministry, or assuring of his prayers for those to whom he writes. In four of his letters, he records the essence of his prayer for them. (Cf. Eph. 1:17-19;3:16-19; Phil. 1:9-11; Col. 1:9-12; II Thess. 1:11, 12). It is interesting to note that, while there are some of them he knows, probably the greater number are Christians whom he has never seen. Yet he prayed for them. His prayers are superb examples of the way to pray wisely and specifically for fellow Christians of whom we may know nothing. In spiritual terms, Paul reaches no greater heights anywhere than in the contents of his prayers for others. It is instructive to note the objectives for which Paul prays. The four prayers are somewhat similar. In the Ephesian letter he wrote: "... *that the God of our Lord Jesus Christ,*

What Is Intercessory Prayer? 97

the Father of glory, may give you a spirit of wisdom and of revelation in the knowledge of Him ... that the eyes of your heart may be enlightened, so that you will know what is the hope of His calling, what are the riches of the glory of His inheritance in the saints, and what is the surpassing greatness of His power toward us who believe"(1:17-19) "...that He would grant you, according to the riches of His glory, to be strengthened with power through His Spirit in the inner man, so that Christ may dwell in your hearts through faith; and that you, being rooted and grounded in love, may be able to comprehend with all the saints what is the breadth and length and height and depth, and to know the love of Christ which surpasses knowledge, that you may be filled up to all the fullness of God." (Eph. 3:16-19 NASB).

To the Philippian church he wrote, *"And this I pray, that your love may abound still more and more in real knowledge and all discernment, so that you may approve the things that are excellent, in order to be sincere and blameless until the day of Christ; having been filled with the fruit of righteousness which comes through Jesus Christ, to the glory and praise of God" (Phil. 1:9-11 NASB).*

To the church at Colossae he sent these words, *"...we have not ceased to pray for you and to ask that you may be filled with the knowledge of His will in all spiritual wisdom and understanding, so that you will walk in a manner worthy of the Lord, to please Him in all respects, bearing fruit in every good work and increasing in the knowledge of God; strengthened with all power, according to His glorious might, for the attaining of all steadfastness and patience (Col. 1:9-11 NASB).*

The prayer for the church at Thessalonica is brief, but similar, *"... we pray for you always, that our God will count you worthy of your calling and fulfill every desire for goodness and the work of faith with power, so that the name of our Lord Jesus will be glorified in you and you in Him" (II Thess. 1:11, 12 NASB).*

No doubt some of these to whom Paul writes were in dire economic straits, or were suffering persecution, but his prayers are primarily for the spiritual needs of fellow believers. He was certainly not unconcerned about their physical needs. He was doubtless aware of some who were being persecuted, and of others who were making great sacrifices for their faith. But his passion was for the Kingdom of

God, and the place of fellow believers in that Kingdom. It was that passion which generated his prayers.

Paul's motivation for his prayers such as these was the wonderful salvation our God provides for us in Christ. He wants his readers to experience the fullness of that salvation, and enjoy the full bounty of their inheritance in Christ. It is tragic that so many professing Christians know so little of what is to them, unfortunately, the unexplored range and riches of God's grace and spiritual blessings. In God's economy, we are much more likely to search for the treasures of God's grace when we see how Paul describes them, and we realize these are objectives we ought to have when we engage in 'intercessory' prayer. To that end, it is important to note how specific the apostle is in what he asks. He didn't blunderbuss or scattershot his prayers. He knew exactly what his fellow believers needed – and this is what he desired for God to bestow on them.

Those for whom Paul prayed had already received the Holy Spirit as the divine seal and mark. He wants them to receive the heavenly wisdom and revelation of God's will and purpose, which will open to them the fullness of the truth of God's Word. We can know nothing spiritually except as God reveals it to us through His Word. The Holy Spirit speaks to us directly at times, but He gives us no eternal truths beyond those already revealed in God's Word. These He will illuminate and open up to us. Jesus said, *"He will guide you into all the truth; for He will not speak on His own initiative, but whatever He hears He will speak; and He will disclose to you what is to come. He will glorify Me, for He will take of Mine, and will disclose it to you" (John 16:13, 14 NASB).* The Christian has no excuse for ignorance – God's Word is given, and the Spirit will interpret it. Paul is not asking for tools of knowledge to be given. His desire is that those for whom he prays may have a wise and understanding spirit. The ultimate outcome is an intimate knowledge of God, and the multiple gifts which are ours through faith in Christ. Surely, there is nothing more greatly needed. As we pray for others, this ought to be high on the list of requests.

In summation, Paul prays for fellow Christians to be given wisdom and understanding, and abound in knowledge and discernment;

to be strengthened with the power of God in the inner person; to know the wonder of the love of God revealed in Christ; to have a view of the riches of the inheritance in store for the faithful; to be counted worthy of the calling extended to us; and be filled with the fruits of righteousness.

We, too, can ask God for all those blessings to be poured out on fellow believers whether we know them or not, and we ought not sin against God in failing to do what we can do. Here are a few suggestions that might be helpful:

Pray intelligently. Find out as much as possible about the needs of the person for whom you pray. God knows those needs already, but you can be more effective if you know what to ask.

Pray for the person by name, if possible. If the individual is a family member, a friend, or an acquaintance, that will be no problem. But if, for instance, you desire to pray for our missionaries, to learn any facts may require a bit of effort. Find names and addresses, then write to that person or persons telling them of your interest and concern – ask them to send you information as to their specific needs. Then you will know how to pray.

Pastors and spiritual leaders carry a tremendous spiritual load. Satan does not worry about people who are willingly involved in sinful activities; they do not need his help or encouragement. So he aims his darts at those who are his strongest opposition – pastors, preachers, elders, deacons, teachers, leaders. He will do all in his power to tempt, try and discourage them. Intercessory prayer is a powerful weapon in the war against the forces of evil. Pray for these fellow Christians that they may be strengthened in the inner person, and as Paul put it, *"With all prayer and petition pray at all times in the Spirit ... be on the alert with all perseverance and petition for all the saints, and pray on my behalf ... that I may speak boldly ... " (Eph. 6:18-20 NASB).*

It is important for us to remember in all our prayers that God's will must be the containing parameter, and His glory should be the ultimate objective.

Don't ignore the fact that the person for whom you pray also has a responsibility. God will not run roughshod over any body to accomplish His will. And we should never prostitute prayer by asking for anything that would in no way honor and glorify God.

Eleven

Is Church Necessary?

ONE MIGHT ASK, "Do I have to be active in church for my prayers to be answered?" The seemingly obvious answer to that question is "No, the church is not essential for prayer." Prayer is an individual function. By far the greatest portion of real praying does not take place in the church as an organization, or in its formal activities. The Scripture teaches us that every person must give an account of himself or herself, and by that same principle, every person must do his or her own praying.

At the same time, the Scripture also teaches us that God does not plan for Christians to operate as lone rangers. If a person has been truly saved from the ravages and penalties of sin through faith in Jesus Christ, the Scripture clearly teaches that such a one has been baptized into Christ, and is part of the body of Christ, which is the church (Cf. I Cor. 12:12, 13, 27; 10:16, 17; Eph. 4:12; Col. 1:18: 2:12). If you truly believe in Jesus Christ as the divine Son of God, Lord of all, and your Savior, then you are part of the church, which is the body of Christ. He is the Head, and thus, the authority. But each of us, as a believer, has a function in the church (Cf. I Cor. 12:12-31). Paul is quite explicit that, as the human body is made up of many parts, each with its own particular place and specific function, the church also is made up of many persons, each of whom has his or her own particular place and function. A vital part of that responsibility is concern for and the care of all the other members (Cf. I Cor. 12:14-27). A primary responsibility is to pray for one another.

As we think about this facet of the Christian life, we are mindful that the institutional church – the church as we have known it – seems to be in the process of rapid and significant changes. There is even the talk that we are in a post-Christian, post-church, era. Some are saying that if the church survives at all, it will be in dramatically different forms.

Contributing to the situation confronting us is the fact that many of the younger generation seem to think of the church only as a provider – a source of benefit to them – offering fellowship, encouragement, helping self-esteem, teaching children good habits, et al. At the same time, others are wondering if the church is really important - is it something that belongs to past generations, but is now passé. Others think of the spiritual life as ultra personal, so why is the church necessary – they argue that one can worship anywhere. So – one might ask, Do I need the church in order to have a satisfying prayer experience?

The Greek word *ECCLESIA* which is translated "church" is used in the New Testament with four basic meanings. Its original meaning was simply "an assembly" or "a group called together for some specific purpose." The New Testament Christians took the word and adapted it to their use as "an assembly of believers." It wound up being used as a term to incorporate all Christians. It was in this latter sense that Jesus spoke when He said, "I will build My church."

In most instances the word in the New Testament means a local group of believers; e.g. the church in Corinth, or Philippi, et al. But the word "church" has come to mean something quite different in our day. In the New Testament to speak of a 'church" meant a group of people everyone of whom claimed a relationship to the body solely because of faith in Jesus Christ. There was no particular emphasis on locality. The "church" in Ephesus, or Antioch, or many other places, might be made up of many "house churches." There was no central gathering place such as a building designated as "the church."

There was little or no effort to operate or perpetuate an institution. It was primarily a fellowship made possible by a common faith in Jesus Christ as Lord and Savior. Organization was minimal, if at all.

The real "church" back then and the real "church" today was, and is, unseen. In the early church there would have been no question about the relationship between prayer and the fellowship. Prayer for those early Christians was a binding tie, uniting them in one great effort – to exalt their Lord and extend His Kingdom.

The Bible clearly teaches that the ultimate objective of prayer is the Kingdom of God. Jesus taught us that we are to ask for the necessities of life – "daily bread" – but He was emphatic that we are to *"seek first the kingdom of God and His righteousness ..."*(Matt. 6:33). He also said *"...if two of you agree on earth about anything that they may ask, it shall be done for them by My Father who is in heaven. For where two or three are gathered together in My name, there I am in their midst"* (Matt. 18:20). To meet with another believer in Jesus' name is not a formality, though the result is the 'church.' The 'church' is the body of Christ, and He says where even two or three persons come together in His name, He is there –He is the Head, and they are the body of the church. For to meet "in His name" is not organizational or procedural – it is purposeful, to do the work He wants done, and accomplish His will. He also declared, *"Abide in Me and I in you. As the branch cannot bear fruit of itself, unless it abides in the vine, so neither can you, unless you abide in Me. I am the vine, you are the branches; he who abides in Me, and I in him, bears much fruit, for apart from Me you can do nothing."* (John 15:4, 5 NASB).

If you are a follower – a disciple – of Christ, your calling is not merely to receive the blessings of God, and be able to latch on to the power of God just for your own purposes. And the privilege of prayer is not for the purpose of getting what you want or need. It is given that you may share in the wonderful business of the Kingdom of God. For that to be possible, you have to be part of the "church" the body of Christ. And your praying, though not limited to the physical closeness of assembly, has to be part of the work of the church of the Lord Jesus.

A crisis in the early church gives us some insight as to the importance of the church. Herod had ordered the death of James, the brother of John. When he saw that this pleased the Jews, he had Peter arrested and put in prison. The church, young and learning, had no difficulty in knowing what it must do. Acts 12:5 tells us that *"constant prayer was offered to God for <u>him by the church"</u>.* The original Greek actually says, "prayer was being offered earnestly (constantly) by the church." Luke gives us no details, but we can be fairly sure he meant the same thing we would mean if we used those same words today: the members of the church prayed individually, but they joined their prayers together as they met as a body to pray.

Your praying as a part of the church is not restricted in any way by the physical operation of the church to which you belong. You can pray any time, anywhere, in any position, or situation. But prayer in some form is an absolute essential in worship. The danger in corporate prayer – a part of the formal worship experience – is that the usual procedure is for one person to voice a prayer, while all the rest of the congregation whether large or small is silent and participate only as auditors. Genuine prayer is work. It is not a lazy person's activity. It requires a focused, intense attention to the matter at hand. A casual, lackadaisical attitude does not lend itself to prayer. It is so easy to be a mere auditor. Yet genuine worship demands that every person in the congregation shall be as intense in prayer as the one who vocalizes his or her words. There can be no worship without prayer of some sort. Praise can take several forms, but any communication with God Himself is prayer. There can be effort, even fervent effort and activity, but Jesus is clear in His statement that nothing in the Kingdom can be accomplished without His participation. That applies fully to prayer. Even fellowship is greatly enriched and blessed when it is enveloped and infused with a pervading spirit of prayer.

There is great power in corporate prayer. Jesus' promise to be where two or three gather in His name implies that He not only will be present, but He will acknowledge them as His followers, and bless them with His intercession as they pray. The early disciples took Him at His word. After Jesus' ascension back to heaven, the disciples gathered in an upper room. Their activity is disclosed by Scripture: *"These all with one mind were continually devoting themselves to prayer. ."* (Acts 1:14 NASB). As a result of their praying they were led to replace Judas with Matthias. It seems evident they continued praying over a period of time, up until the Day of Pentecost. When that day came, the power of God came down in the Person of the Holy Spirit, and a mighty response took place when Peter preached to the multitude that had gathered there in Jerusalem. There was a "sound from heaven" and all that great crowd, who had come from many different lands, heard, each person in his or her own language, the message from God through the disciples.

Following that experience, there were many times when the church met for the specific purpose of prayer. They had learned that God heard and answered when they prayed as a body of believers. A church which does not engage often in earnest prayer is a dead church. In a real sense, prayer is the main business of a congregation. God is not limited when His people fail to pray – He is free to do what He wills to do. But at the same time, He resolutely keeps off limits any person or group deliberately ignoring the privilege of an audience with Him in prayer.

It should be obvious that the church in no way displaces the individual's need in prayer. Without individuals who pray, the church is voiceless. At the same time, it should be clear that an individual's privilege of prayer is closely intertwined with being a part of the body of Christ, the church. When Paul wrote to the various churches asking them to pray for him, he was thinking, surely, of individuals praying, both as part of the church, and in their times of purely personal prayer. But his emphasis was on their cooperation and unity in a single object of prayer – Paul and his ministry.

An individual can worship God all alone. Worship is the physical, mental and spiritual acknowledgement of God as who He is – the Creator and source of all that exists, and who upholds it all by His power. It is yearning to "hallow" the name of our God in all our words and work. The emphasis in the mind of the worshipper is God, not self. Worship is the conscious effort to communicate to God the inner desire that His name be honored and glorified. But we normally think of worship as a corporate experience – people in a group (size is meaningless) sharing in the expression of their devotion to and reverence for God. Even so, the act of worship is, by its very nature, an individual activity and exercise. Though a vast crowd may be involved in what we call worship, everyone of whom may share in the blessings of that experience, each individual in that crowd is totally responsible if real worship takes place. No one can worship for another. For worship itself is not a physical activity. It is the most secret agenda of the human soul – it takes place in the deepest recesses of one's being. But that same individuality means that one may be sitting, or standing, in the midst of a worshipping congregation and be as far from God as if sitting in a bar, or watching a lewd movie. It is the individual who is truly the temple of God (Cf. I Cor. 3:16).

It ought to be evident that only a person in the right relationship with God can pray and expect God to hear and answer. And that relationship is completely dependent upon one's faith in Jesus Christ as the divine Son of God who was born of the virgin Mary, lived a sinless life, died on a cross to pay the penalty for the sins of those who believe in Him, and rose from the dead to justify the salvation of believers, and now sits at the right hand of God the Father interceding for those who have faith in Him. The Scriptures clearly teach that those who have that kind of faith are IN Christ, and are part of the body of Christ which is the church.

Anyone who deliberately separates himself or herself from the church, the body of Christ, is automatically shutting one's self off from effective prayer. What can you pray for if there is no concern for the Kingdom of God? There is nothing left except personal, selfish desires. James is emphatic saying, *"You ask and do not receive, because you ask with the wrong motives so that you may spend it on your pleasures … do you not know that friendship with the world is hostility toward God? Therefore whoever wishes to be a friend of the world makes himself an enemy of God. Or do you think that the Scripture speaks to no purpose:* "He *jealously desires the Spirit which He has made to dwell in us?"* (James 4:3-5 NASB).

All of the prayers acceptable to God move ultimately to one end and purpose – the complete establishment of God's Kingdom. In writing to Timothy, Paul uses four different words to indicate varieties of prayer: (1) supplications, or entreaties – petitions for felt needs; (2) prayers – they may be petitions, but generally mean any form of address directed to God. A small child was standing at a window on a beautiful morning talking. Her mother asked, "To whom are you talking?" The child said "To God." The mother then asked, "What are you asking Him for?" The child replied, "Nothing. I'm just talking to Him." It is not hard to feel that God might like more of that kind. (3) intercessions – the word in its basic meaning indicates 'freedom of access' so that one is in the very audience-chamber of God, talking to God in behalf of others. (4) thanksgivings – a full awareness of God's multiple, bountiful blessings should bring us to our knees in humble gratitude.

Paul says that all of these are to be *"made on behalf of all men, for kings and for all who are in authority"*, and the reason is general welfare, *"that we may lead a tranquil and quiet life in all godliness and dignity"* (I Tim. 2:2 NASB). Paul is saying that we are to pray for our public leaders so the situation may offer openness to godliness.

This kind of praying can, and should be, done by the individual Christian in his or her solitude. But Paul is telling Timothy that this is the kind of praying to be done in the church. His mindset surely is that the individual Christian will be involved in both kinds of praying – alone and in the company of fellow believers.

Twelve

Is Anything Off Limits?

JESUS SAID, "*IF YOU abide in Me, and My words abide in you, ask whatever you wish, and it shall be done for you*" (John 15:7 NASB). Is Jesus opening wide the door so I can ask for anything I want? Or is there some hidden restriction set up by Jesus' words? Does God say some things are definitely off limits? What are the parameters in force in this business of praying?

In one sense, there is nothing off limits. We can ask for anything we may wish. People sometimes pray for strange and unusual things. A lady who lived alone except for her dog called her pastor one day. He could tell by the tone and intensity of her voice that she was quite upset; she was actually crying. He asked her what her problem was, and she told him that her little dog was sick, and the veterinarian had told her the dog might not recover. She wanted the pastor to pray for her dog. There are far more exotic requests for prayer than this. But we normally do not think of bothering God with such requests. But the question is real – are some things off limits?

When we begin to think of the range of things for which prayer is justified perhaps we should ask the question, What is the basic purpose for which God has given us the privilege of prayer? Is it basically just a tool to help us with our needs? Is it primarily a means of communication by which we let God know what our wants and needs may be? It appears that the great majority of people have a concept of prayer which combines the two. Many people think of it somewhat like a direct telephone line to God by which we can call Him whenever we need help.

The word 'pray' comes to us by way of several changes from the old Latin "precarious" which meant "uncertain,' or "without foundation." It meant something one had no real claim to receive, but for which one pled or begged. It was a request for something which could be obtained no other way. A mother whose only son, a soldier in the French army, had been court-martialed for negligence on duty, and condemned to execution, came to Napoleon ask for her son's reprieve. Napoleon looked over the records, then said, "Madam, I find that your son was guilty of inexcusable neglect; he deserves no reprieve." On her knees, she said, "Your majesty, I did not come to claim any merit. I came only to pray for your mercy for my only son."

Early Biblical prayer retains something of that idea. But by the time we reach the teaching of Jesus and the New Testament, the concept of prayer is greatly enlarged. In fact, in the early pages of the Old Testament, prayer is not mentioned. We find no instance of any kind of prayer until we get to Abraham. In Genesis 13 we read that after Abraham returned from Egypt, he went back to the place where he had been when he first entered Canaan, between Bethel and Ai, *"to the place of the altar which he had made there first. And there Abram called on the name of the Lord"* (Gen. 13:4 NKJV).

In Genesis 17, God tells Abraham that Sarai will bear a son in her old age. Abraham converses with God about the matter. When the conversation is finished we read, *"And when He finished talking with him, God went up from Abraham"* (17:22 NASB). In those early days, communication between God and those He chose to hear was simple conversation, as shown when Abraham interceded with God in behalf of Sodom (Cf. Gen. 18:22-33).

In the New Testament, petition is clearly indicated as a vital part of prayer. But we do need to discern if there is any limit specifically declared. Does God restrict us to only certain areas? What does the Scripture tell us about this?

Jesus' commands and Instructions

When the disciples asked the Lord to teach them to pray, they were surely interested in more than the form of prayer – what to say, when and where. We may assume justifiably that they were concerned as to the content – what they could pray for. In the Model Prayer, Jesus gave vital instructions as to both form and content.

We have discussed the Model Prayer earlier. But a brief look at it won't hurt. There are six petitions in this prayer, divided into two groups. The first three concern God and His Kingdom, while the other three involve Kingdom subjects and personal needs. We know from other parts of the Scriptures, and personal experience, that Jesus was in no way limiting prayer by giving us the Model Prayer. He knew even better than we that there are other areas of need. He was giving us a pattern which can be enlarged.

We know in our hearts that there are desires which are not appropriate as objects of prayer for the true disciple of Christ. Yet, in reality, God decrees no basic prohibitions. He told Jeremiah, "*. . do not pray for this people, and do not lift up cry or prayer for them ...*"(Jer. 7:16 NASB). But that was in response to a particular situation. We would normally think that it would be foolish to pray for a million dollars. But there can be a time when it is well within God's will for such a prayer. A church needed some additional property. The cost for purchase and renovation was $1,250,000. The pastor counseled with the congregation, asking them not to go in debt, but to raise the necessary funds before purchase was made. He asked them to pray and give the $1,250,000. The result was complete success. Many in that congregation prayed that God would enable them to raise that sum and He heard their prayer.

God is not likely to hear a prayer for a Cadillac. But there may be many times when a believer humbly asks God to provide transportation of some sort, and God hears and provides. What is the difference? The difference is in the purpose of the request. The prayer for a

Cadillac is likely to be purely selfish, while the prayer for transportation may fit quite well in God's plans.

Jesus gave other instructions as to what we should ask in prayer. In the 12th chapter of Luke He is very specific in telling us we are not to be overly concerned about material things. He begins by urging His disciples not to be afraid of persecution which harms the body and may cause death. He says, *"And I say to you," My friends, do not be afraid of those who kill the body ..."* (Lk 12:4a NASB). The basis for such courage and boldness is the assurance of God's care. He declares that not even a sparrow is forgotten before God, and adds, *"Indeed, the very hairs of your head are all numbered. Do not fear; you are of more value than many sparrows"* (Lk. 12:7 NASB).

Then having told the parable of the rich man who built bigger barns, He gave specific instructions. We are not to worry about what we will eat or wear. God feeds the birds, and we are of far more value than these. Nor are we to worry about clothing. God clothes the grass and arrays the lilies. Jesus poses the question, *"... how much more will He clothe you, O men of little faith!"* (Lk. 12:28b NASB). He sums up His teaching on this by saying, *"... your Father knows that you need these things. But seek for His kingdom, and these things shall be added to you ... for your Father has chosen gladly to give you the kingdom "* (Lk. 12:30b-32 NASB).

Jesus also gave instruction as to three things we are to pray for. Rather than concentrate on the physical and material needs we have, or desire, we are to ask for the Holy Spirit to be given to us in power. He says, *"If you then, being evil, know how to give good gifts to your children, how much more shall your Heavenly Father give the Holy Spirit to those who ask Him?"*(Luke 11:13 NASB). His point is, if you know how to provide what is best for your children, then surely God knows how to give you not only what is a necessity, but what is the greatest blessing. The emphasis, of course, is that we are to pray for what is most important in life – the gift and guidance of the Holy Spirit. James also further emphasizes this object of prayer. Any intelligent person knows that wisdom is the most valuable component of our mental and spiritual equipment. So James advises, *"But if any of you lacks wisdom, let him ask of God, who gives to all generously and without reproach, and it will be given to him*" (James 1:5 NASB). That is a wonderful statement. If we really want wisdom, all we have to do is ask God for it. That is a prayer every true Christian ought to gladly, eagerly pray.

Jesus also tells us we are to pray for God to provide workers for the harvest of souls. He looked out on the multitude of people, and saw them as so weary and "scattered." He was moved with compassion. Then He said to the disciples, *"The harvest is plentiful, but the workers are few. Therefore beseech the Lord of the harvest to send out workers into His harvest."* (Matt. 9: 37, 38 NASB). He wants us to have the same compassion that possessed Him. And He wants us to have the same concern for the Kingdom. It is a privilege to share with God - Father, Son and Holy Spirit – as principals in the Kingdom. We are to inherit the Kingdom, but at this moment, it exists for each of us only as we have made Jesus Lord and King of our lives. It is our privilege, opportunity and responsibility to help extend that Kingdom by bringing others into a similar relationship with God. If that is the top priority in our lives, then we will surely be diligent in praying, as He has taught us, that the Kingdom will come in full fruition, and that laborers will be plentiful for the harvest God desires.

A third important object of prayer Jesus points out to us is that we will not fall into temptation. As Jesus led His disciples to the Garden of Gethsemane on the night before His crucifixion, He said to them, *"Keep watching and praying, that you may not enter into temptation."* (Matt. 26:41 NASB) It was sorely needed that night. But it is always a need. Temptation is all around us, and ever confronting us. This prayer ought to be a staple item for us.

Lessons from Paul

Jesus, of course, is our Master Teacher in the school of prayer. But Paul also has some valuable lessons for us. When we are thinking about the basic purposes of prayer, and the things we ought to pray for, Paul is a good example and pattern for us to follow. In his letters there are seventeen instances where he reveals to us his own prayers, or his requests to his readers for prayer. An unusual similarity is found

Is Anything Off Limits?   113

in all these. Nowhere does he pray for, or ask his readers to pray for, his material, physical well being except as it relates to his ability to do what he is called to do. Almost all of these prayers and requests for prayer center on one thing – his effectiveness in preaching the Gospel, or the effectiveness of his readers in living the Christian life.

In Romans 1:8-12 he prays that the way may be opened for him to come to Rome to encourage his fellow believers and strengthen them in the faith. His only request for himself is that in this he himself may be encouraged.

In Romans 15:13 he prays that his readers may be filled with joy and peace, and overflow with hope by the power of the Holy Spirit.

In I Cor. 1:4 he thanks God for the grace that has been given to the believers in Corinth.

In II Cor. 8:16 he thanks God for giving to Titus the same concern for the Christians at Corinth as that which he feels. *"But thanks be to God who puts the same earnestness on your behalf in the heart of Titus."* (NASB). Paul expresses his gratitude to God that He has given to Titus the same compassionate concern for the Christians in Corinth as Paul had in his preaching the Gospel there, and that this fellow missionary is there to minister to them.

In Ephesians 1:15-19 the Apostle thanks God for the people of this region, and prays that they may have the spirit of wisdom and revelation in the knowledge of Jesus; that they may know God better, and that they may be enlightened to know fully the hope that God gives to His faithful children. Paul asks that they might know the riches of the glory of God's inheritance in those who are His saints, and the marvelous greatness of His power toward those who believe.

Then in Eph.3:14-19 he prays that they may come to know the immeasurable riches of God's love in Christ – that inner spiritual strength which comes through the indwelling Christ and the power of the Holy Spirit. He desires that they may know the wonderful fullness of the Love of Christ – *"the width and length and depth and height"* (3:18 NKJV), and thus be filled with the fullness of God. That cannot mean all of God, but it does mean all that one can experience of the love, the power, the grace and the wisdom of God.

For the church at Colossae he prayed that they might be filled with the knowledge of the will of God, so as to lead a life worthy of the Lord – a life pleasing to the Lord, and bearing fruit, as they found strength for endurance and patience (Cf. Col. 1:9-12). Then he asked them to pray that God would open the door for him to proclaim the message and mystery of Christ, and proclaim it clearly (Cf. 4:2-4).

He gave thanks for the faithfulness of the Thessalonians (1:2, 3), and expressed his prayer that he might see them again, and that God would clear the way. But he also prayed that their love for each other would increase, and that they would be strengthened in their hearts so as to be blameless and holy in the presence of the Lord at His return (Cf. I Thess. 3:10-13).

Three times in his second letter to the Thessalonians, he expresses his prayer for them. First, he prayed that God would count them worthy of His calling, and by His power enable them to fulfill their Spirit inspired desires so that the name of Jesus would be glorified (Cf. II Thess. 1:11, 12). In his second prayer he asked that the Lord would direct their hearts into God's love and the patience of Christ (3:5). The third prayer was that the Lord of peace would give them peace. (3:16).

To the Philippians he expressed his thanksgiving to God for their fellowship in the Gospel (1:3-6) and then prayed that their love would abound in knowledge and discernment so that they might always make the right choices, and thus be pure and blameless, filled with the fruit of righteousness(Cf. 1:9-11).

When Paul wrote to Timothy, he urged Timothy and those with him to pray for all those in authority so that a quiet and peaceable life in godliness and reverence might be secured (Cf. I Tim. 2:1-3, 8). For himself, he thanked the Lord Jesus that he had been chosen and enabled to be in the ministry of the Gospel (Cf. I Tim. 1:12). In his second letter to Tmothy he thanked God for the memories he had of Timothy and his family, and prayed that he might have an opportunity to see them again. He also prayed that God would grant mercy to Onesiphorus and his family (Cf. II Tim. 1:3, 16-18). Then he prayed that God would grant to Timothy understanding in all things (Cf. 2:7).

In his brief letter to Philemon, he prayed that his friend might be active in sharing his faith, and have full understanding of all the many blessings we have in Christ (Cf. Philemon 4-6).

It is also worth noting that the writer of Hebrews prays that his readers will be equipped with everything needed to do the will of God, and achieve what is pleasing to Him (Cf. Heb. 13:21). And James urges his readers to pray for wisdom, and tells them that when one is ill,, the elders are to pray over that person (Cf. James 1:5-8; 5:14). Note, too, that John prayed for the good health, physically and spiritually, of his readers (Cf. 3 John 2).

The Bible does not actually put any limitation on what we can ask of God. Jesus clearly teaches us that we are to pray for fulfillment of our physical, material needs as they occur, but He also is very specific that we are not to worry about what we eat, or drink, or wear. And it is very clear that He has put limits on what He will grant. And we are given to understand that in God's great plan for the redemption of sinful humanity, and the ultimate extension of His Kingdom, His desire is that we share with Him in His divine purposes.

Jesus tells us to pray for our daily food. James instructs the elders to pray for those sick. John prays for the good health and prosperity of his friends. But the great majority of the prayers, and information about prayer, in the New Testament deals with purely spiritual matters. If we are to follow that example, then what we learn from the Scriptures, is that it is justifiable for us to pray for our personal physical needs, but that the great emphasis in our praying should be for the work of the Kingdom of God. We have the privilege of praying for healing when family members or friends are sick. We are to pray for more laborers in the Kingdom, and we are to ask God's blessings – His wisdom, guidance, strength and provisions – for all who serve Him. We are also to ask God to help us be of greater usefulness in the kingdom, and to guide us in all that is needed for the task which is ours.

James helps us to find the right spirit and motive in all our praying with his warning, *"You ask and do not receive, because you ask with wrong motives, so that you may spend it on your pleasures"* (4:3 NASB). God has no interest in helping us enjoy the luxuries of life. His primary concern is for His own glory, the exaltation of our Lord Jesus Christ, and the extension of His Kingdom. Yet withal, in His gracious love toward us, He wants to do for us all we need as His children. If an earnest prayer is not answered, it is because the answer is not in the will of God, or else that He has something better in store for us.

Section III – What Makes It Work?

In this portion, we will look at what the Bible teaches are essential factors in an effective prayer life. These are the attitudes and actions which must be present and active for our prayers to be acceptable to God.

13. Trust and Loving Obedience
14. Ask in Jesus' Name
15. Staying with the Bible
16. Persistence
17. Depending on the Holy Spirit
18. Sharing in the Kingdom of God

Thirteen

Trust and Loving Obedience

IT IS OBVIOUS THAT real prayer is possible only as one who prays has faith in the One to whom prayer is made. But this faith is more than mental belief. James tells us, *"You believe that God is one. You do well; the demons also believe, and shudder"*(James 2:19 NASB). Simply to believe that God exists, and that He is able to answer prayer, is not enough. Job's words express total trust, "Though He slay me, yet will I trust Him"(13:15 NKJV). This is the essence of trust. It is to be willing to put one's self in God's hand without reservation. He spoke through Isaiah saying, *"But he who puts his trust in Me shall possess the land and shall inherit My holy mountain"*(57:13c NASB).

What is this business of 'trust'? One friend might say of another, "I would trust him with all I have." Or, "I would trust him with my life." What does that mean? Is it not that the one speaking is saying, "I am willing to accept whatever that friend does any time, in any situation" ?

To fully trust God is to be willing to accept as good whatever God does. It is to be willing to accept whatever answer He may give to your prayer. It is to believe wholeheartedly in those words, *"And we know that God causes all things to work together for good to those who love*

God, to those who are called according to His purpose" (Rom. 8:28 NASB). God does not promise us that everything which happens will be good. Problems will arise; difficulties will appear; troubles will surface in every life. God does not promise to rid us of our problems. But He does promise that for those who put their trust in Him He will use every iota of a situation for their good. He will take every part of a situation, the good and the bad, and cause it to produce something good. And in all of it, He also promises that He will never leave us. And He does tell us through Paul, *"Be anxious for nothing, but in everything by prayer and supplication with thanksgiving let your requests be made known to God"* (Phil. 4:6 NASB). If we put our full trust in God, we will never need to worry or be anxious. When we pray, we can be confident of the result. It may not be answered exactly as we request, but because of our trust in our God, we can be sure His answer will be the best possible. His word to those who are truly His is, *"It will also come to pass that before they call, I will answer; and while they are still speaking, I will hear"* (Isa. 65:24 NASB). And hear these wonderful words, *"Because he has loved Me, therefore I will deliver him. ... He will call upon Me, and I will answer him; I will be with him in trouble; I will rescue him, and honor him"* (Ps. 91:14, 15 NASB).

The evidence of real trust is full obedience. A missionary had taught his children to obey his commands exactly. There are those who would say that this was going way overboard. But one day his little boy was playing outside, and the father saw that a cobra was within striking distance of the child. His word to the child was "Don't move!" If the child had moved before he could give the command, or if he moved in disobedience to the command, the viper would have bitten him, and death might have resulted. But because the child had been taught to obey his father's commands exactly, he never moved, and the father was able to draw the snake away from his son.

Small children learn obedience through discipline. But as a person grows older, love becomes the motivation for obedience. Babes in Christ may be at the stage where obedience is a shadowy consciousness of the authority of God. But as one grows and matures in Christian knowledge and grace, obedience to our Lord's teaching and commands becomes the response of love. And through experience we learn that God can be fully trusted. Consequently, our prayer life becomes an activity of communication through which our requests are primarily an acknowledgment of our need and God's abundant provision. Even as we make those requests we yield to a loving Father's wisdom and grace in willing obedience.

Moses warned the people of Israel as they were preparing to go into the Promised Land, *"Beware lest you forget the Lord your God by not keeping His commandments and His ordinances and His statutes ...Like the nations that the Lord makes to perish before you, so you shall perish because you would not listen to the voice of the Lord your God"* (Deut. 8:11, 20 NASB; Cf. Deut. 11;28). In Deut. 13:4 Moses declared, *"You shall follow the Lord your God and fear Him; and you shall keep His commandments, listen to His voice, serve Him, and cling to Him"* Dozens of times in the Old Testament, God spoke the same message to the people through His prophets. When David installed his son, Solomon, as king, his words to Solomon were wise, *"Only the Lord give you discretion and understanding ... so that you may keep the law of the Lord your God. Then you shall prosper, if you are careful to observe the statutes and ordinances which the Lord commanded Moses concerning Israel"* (I Chron. 22:12, 13 NASB). Through Jeremiah God spoke, *"They have turned back to the iniquities of their ancestors who refused to hear My words ... . though they will cry to Me, yet I will not listen to them ... .Therefore do not pray for this people, nor lift up a cry or prayer for them, for I will not listen when they call to Me because of their disaster"* (11:10, 11, 14 NASB). Through the Prophet Isaiah God said, *"If you consent and obey, you will eat the best of the land ..."* (1:19 NASB). But He also spoke of their disobedience and sinfulness and said, *"So when you spread out your hands in prayer I will hide My eyes from you, yes even though you multiply prayers, I will not listen"* (1:15 NASB).

Jesus said to His followers, *"If you love Me, you will keep My commandments."* (John 14:15 NASB). I believe His emphasis was on the word 'will'. The result of the verb 'love' is obedience. The inner meaning of the word 'love' is the giving of one's self to another. That is submissiveness. If a man loves a woman to the point that he wants her for his wife, his love is not merely what appears on the surface – the desire to possess her as his own. It is also the desire to give himself to her. That involves obedience to her wishes and desires.

How much more true is the result of our love for God. Jesus' commandment is summed up in two parts: (1) "YOU SHALL LOVE THE LORD YOUR GOD WITH ALL YOUR HEART, AND WITH ALL YOUR SOUL, AND WITH ALL YOUR MIND"; and (2) "YOU SHALL LOVE YOUR NEIGHBOR AS YOURSELF"(Matt. 22:37, 39) – I am sure Jesus knew full well that for any of us ordinary human beings, perfect obedience to those commandments is impossible. But the will to obey is easily apparent. For those two commandments sum up all the commandments of God and the teaching of Jesus.

There are only two possible attitudes toward the commandments of God and the laws of a nation. The usual human attitude is rebellion – how can I escape the networking of the legal system, and how can I get by without yielding to the restrictions and limiting power of those commandments? But the attitude of those who have been called by God, and have been brought into a close relationship with Him, is that of a child who dearly loves his/her parents and wants to please them. The true child of God *wills* to be obedient.

Such obedience is an essential factor in effective praying. If you were planning to ask the City Mayor for a favor but you had broken some of the laws, and had made it evident that you did not agree with him in his plans and his actions, what would be the chances of his looking kindly toward your request? A father had asked his teen age son to do a special task. The boy had failed to do as his father asked. When he, then, asked his Dad for something he wanted, the father said, "Son, you have not done the job I asked you to do. I don't think I'll have any reason to do what you want." God is not a weak and prejudicial human being, but the same principle applies. God is not going to be interested in some need or project which runs contrary to His own purposes and plans. Those who love the Lord as Jesus has quoted, and whose spirit is that of obedience and submissiveness, will not knowingly pray for something contrary to the will of God. Jesus set the example for us when He prayed, *"Not My will but Thine be done"* That is the spirit of obedience.Because of our humanity, much of our praying will naturally involve our human needs and desires. We are taught to pray for food, to pray for forgiveness and deliverance from evil. We are also encouraged to pray for fellow Christians – their physical and spiritual needs and opportunities. Prayers of these kinds will occupy much of our prayer time. There is nothing wrong with this, provided they do not completely dominate our effort. We must not forget that Jesus' instruction by means of the Model Prayer starts with this emphasis, *"Hallowed be Thy Name; Thy kingdom come; Thy will be done on ea rth as it is in heaven"* Jesus is clearly teaching us that God's will, His purpose and plans, His desires are all more important than our needs, even our spiritual needs.

Trust in God will enable us to be willingly, even gladly obedient to Him in every way, and to express that trust in all our praying. In whatever we ask for, we should be fully trusting in that we recognize without question that God's answer is the best answer. Whether He gives or withholds, we will be grateful – that is trust.

Fourteen

Ask in Jesus' Name

For Christians of an evangelical persuasion, a prayer will usually end with one of two phrases – either "in Jesus' name," or "for Jesus' sake," – or something similar. Have you ever stopped to ponder and ask why those particular phrases are used? The chances are, if you use those phrases, or something similar, that you do it almost automatically, without thinking about the words at all. Why do you use them? Is it of any significance? Are they necessary? Just what do they mean?

It is interesting to note how many times, and for what specific purposes, Jesus used the phrase "In My name," or "for My name's sake," which is the wording in the King James Version. Other versions occasionally translate such into "on account of My name," or "because of Me." Here are a few instances:-

"And you will be hated by all on account of My name" (Matt. 10:22 NASB).

"Whoever receives one such child in My name receives Me" (Matt. 18:5 NASB).

"For where two or three have gathered together in My name, there I am in their midst" (Matt. 18:20 NASB).

"And everyone who has left houses or brothers or sisters or father or mother or children or farms, for My name's sake ... " (Matt. 19:29 NASB).

"For many will come in My name, saying, 'I am the Christ'. and will mislead many" (Matt. 24:5 NASB).

"... .for there is no one who shall perform a miracle in My name, and be able soon afterward to speak evil of Me" (Mark 9:39 NASB).

"... .in My name they will cast out demons ... ." (Mark 16:17 NASB).

Each of these statements has great meaning for believers. They tell us much about this business of being followers and disciples of Jesus Christ. Look at the implications: (1) The very name of Jesus used by those who claim Him as Lord and Savior will cause them to be hated and persecuted;(2) Any help given to those who hold His name as their banner, even so little as a cup of water, when given in His wonderful name, will be rewarded; (3) He honors His name with His presence when even so few as two or three persons gather in and because of His name; (4) Whatever sacrifice is made by those who are followers of Jesus Christ, and because of their loyalty to His name, will be rewarded and repaid; (5) His name is such a magnet that many deceivers will try to use His name; (6) His name is such a power that His followers were able to cast out demons in His name; (7) His name is of such significance that one who is able to work a miracle using His name will not be able to speak evil of Him.

If Jesus was boasting of Himself in human terms, then these statements reveal a true egomaniac. But we know Him, and thus we know there is something of power and eternal value in those words, "in My name," or "for My name's sake." Thus it is important for us to learn the true significance these words have.

But it is when Jesus talks about praying and tells us to pray in His name that we pay closest attention. Six times the Scripture records

Jesus saying to His disciples, "Ask, in My name." All of these are in the Gospel of John. What is the significance of this statement? Perhaps there are many people, even devout Christians, who have never stopped to think seriously about the underlying purpose and meaning of those words. It is so easy to fall into the habit of using the phrase "in Jesus name" as a sort of magic talisman, as if the mere saying of the words generated some mystical power. Is our Lord saying that the mere use of those exact words "in Jesus' name" is the password to the throne of God?

Earnest Christians pay a great deal of attention to the words our Lord spoke during His earthly stay. We study His words, and memorize them, and try to understand them. They have a unique importance for those who are true disciples. When He spoke to His disciples the night before His crucifixion He told them, *"Whatever you ask in My name, that I will do, that the Father may be glorified in the Son. If you ask anything in My name, I will do it"* (John 14:13, 14 NKJV). Those words changed the entire concept of prayer for Christians. If they mean anything, they mean prayer in the name of Jesus Christ has power with God. But is simply speaking those words all that is necessary?

What Do They Mean?

Anyone who has studied the Scriptures seriously knows full well that Jesus certainly did not mean the mere adding of those words "in Jesus' name" at the end of a prayer will result in it being answered as we want it to be. God does not put the key to Heaven's blessings in our hands. Look carefully at John 15:16, *"You did not choose Me, but I chose you, and appointed you that you should go and bear fruit, and that your fruit should remain, that whatever you ask the Father in My name He may give you."(NKJV)*. If those words apply to us today (and we believe they do), then it means our association with Christ is due to His choice, not ours. It also means that anything of worth we may see accomplished is due to His work in us, not just our efforts. He said, *"I am the vine, you are the branches; he who abides in Me, and I in him, he bears much fruit; for apart from Me you can do nothing"* (John 15:5 NASB).

Jesus reveals two purposes in calling and appointing disciples –

first, they are to go – sent to be His emissaries and missionaries wherever they go. How important it is for us who believe in Jesus Christ as our Lord and Saviour to remember that we do not follow our own program and strategy. We do not go on our own initiative; we are sent by Him. The purpose and desired result of our going is to produce fruit, and the fruit is to have a continuing, lasting character. It is not something which is perishable. It is fruit of the Spirit – souls born into the kingdom of God, productivity of many kinds that brings glory to God, because it reproduces the characteristics of Jesus Christ, His Son.

The second purpose of His calling is that His chosen ones may have the privilege of praying to the Father, <u>asking for the things Christ desires of His disciples and their work.</u> This is a divine opportunity to which Jesus calls disciples. On one occasion He urged His disciples, *"Therefore pray the Lord of the harvest to send out laborers into His harvest"* (Matt. 9:38 NKJV). Why should it be necessary to ask the owner to furnish laborers for His harvest? Because those who pray "in Jesus' name" have a vital concern for the harvest. Such a vital concern will produce the "fruit" Jesus desires, and for which His disciples are called. But if the fruit which will "remain" and which will honor the Lord is to be produced then we must ask the Father for it in the Master's name. Jesus taught that we who are His disciples are the "branches" through whom He keeps on "doing the works of God," which is the "fruit" that remains – it does not spoil. Human workers will produce spiritual fruit that has eternal qualities only as God produces it through them. Nothing spoils so quickly and is so useless as diseased, spoiled, rotting fruit. Our self-centered human efforts always produce fruit that is diseased and useless, or worse.

Prayer, therefore, is vital. We are to represent and reproduce the Lord in prayer. We must be able to go to the Father at all times to ask Him for whatever is needed to carry on the work of Christ in the world. The essence of this task is that Christ may be living and visible in us so that our lives will reproduce His life in some small way. Jesus is actually saying "that whatever you shall request of the Father as My representatives, He may give it to you." The guaranty of an answered prayer depends on whether the one praying comes to the Father as a true representative of Christ, and on whether the prayer and its answer will in some way be used of the Lord for the work of His kingdom.

Jesus Is the Only Way to God

The wisdom of the world argues that there are many roads to God, and one is as good as another. It is heart-breaking to see some who claim to be believers in Jesus Christ join the 'universalists' in saying that other religions may be as good for those who hold to them as Christianity is for us who believe in Jesus Christ. God's Word – the living Word, Christ, and the written Word, the Bible – says there is only one way to God and that is through Jesus Christ. Jesus said in the plainest, simplest words, *"I am the way, the truth, and the life. No one comes to the Father except through Me"* (John 14:6 NKJV). Nothing could be any plainer or more exclusive. If His words are truth, then there is no other way to God. Peter reiterates that truth, *"Nor is there salvation in any other, for there is no other name under heaven, given among men, by which we must be saved"* (Acts 4:12 NKJV).

If salvation is only through Christ, then prayer must surely follow the same route. To pray in Jesus' Name is to be aware that we have no right to come to the Father except through Him. The teaching is plain that we have no way to reach the Father except as we come in the Son's name. Unless we consciously come to the Father as believers in Jesus Christ, and thus in His name, we will not be heard.

If I were to go to the White House in Washington and ask for an audience with the President, I would not even get in the gate. But if I were to go far enough that someone would ask me, "What credentials do you have?" I would have to reply, "None." However, if the President had a son, and I knew that son personally because he had rescued me from death, he might take pity on me and say, "If you ever want to get in to see My Father, here is a note that will get you in." With that note, I would have no problem getting into the oval office. It would not happen because of who I am or what I have done, but only because the President's son interceded for me.

Jesus speaks of those of us who have accepted Him as Lord and Savior as His friends. (Cf. John 15:14). We are able to lift up our prayers to the Heavenly Father because we come to Him in the Name of His Son, our Lord. We are able to do that because the Son, our Lord, has told us to seek an audience with the Father through the power of His name.

Jesus Is Our Surrogate in Prayer

One of the most precious promises Jesus made to His disciples is that He will be our surrogate – our deputy or representative- at the throne of God in heaven. The high priest, Eli, upbraiding his sons for their wickedness, said, *"But if a man sins against the Lord, who will intercede for him?"* (I Sam. 2:25 NKJV). That question remained to face mankind until Jesus came. Isaiah foretold the marvelous answer, *"And He bore the sin of many, and made intercession for the transgressors"* (53:12e NKJV). But the promise became reality only when Jesus Himself came and was revealed as the atonement for our sins, and the Savior who would be the Way to God.

The writer of Hebrews tells us, *"Therefore He is able to save to the uttermost those who come to God through Him, since He ever lives to make intercession for them"* (7:25 NKJV). He also says, *"For Christ has not entered the holy places made with hands ... . but into heaven itself, now to appear in the presence of God for us"* (9:24 NKJV). Jesus Himself said, when being interrogated by the Sanhedrin, *"Hereafter the Son of Man will sit on the right hand of the power of God"* (Luke 22:69 NKJV). As Stephen was testifying to the High Priest and Sanhedrin, it is written of him, *"But he, being full of the Holy Spirit, gazed into heaven and saw the glory of God, and Jesus standing at the right hand of God, and said, "Look! I see the heavens opened and the Son of Man standing at the right hand of God"* (Acts 7:55, 56 NKJV).

Our Lord is at the right hand of the Father, sharing in the glory of God. But His purpose there is more than simply to bask in glory or share in power. As our blessed Savior, He is there interceding for those who are His. The writer of Hebrews says, *"Therefore He is able to save to the uttermost those who come to God through Him, since He ever lives* to make intercession for them" (7:25 NKJV). John writes, *"And if anyone sins, we have an Advocate with the Father, Jesus Christ the Righteous"* (I John 2:1b NKJV).

Paul gives us wonderful comfort in these words, *"Likewise the Spirit also helps in our weaknesses. For we do not know what we should pray for as we ought, but the Spirit Himself makes intercession for us with groanings which cannot be uttered.. Now He who searches the hearts knows what the mind of the Spirit is, because He makes intercession for the saints according to the will of God"* (Romans 8:26, 27 NKJV).

We knock on the door of heaven knowing full well we have no credentials of our own, no merit or worth. The basis of our prayer to God is the merit of Jesus Christ, His only begotten Son. He is there pleading our case, interceding in our behalf. At the same time, He expects us to be so identified with Him in the work of the Kingdom here that we will be led by the Holy Spirit to know whether what we pray for is of such nature that God can be glorified in it. Our devotion to Christ should be of such character and quality that even as we pray for physical and material needs of ourselves and others, we will desire God's will to be done, and He will be glorified. Paul gives us those wonderful words, *"For you did not receive the spirit of bondage again to fear, but you received the spirit of adoption by whom we cry out, "Abba, Father." The Spirit Himself bears witness with our spirit that we are children of God, and if children, then heirs ..."* (Romans 8:15-17a NKJV).

God Acts for Jesus' Sake

We come to God, then, not as foreigners asking an audience, but as His adopted children. We are not merely beggars, nor are we just spectators, watching the activities of the Kingdom from the cheapest seats in the balcony. We are citizens of the Kingdom; indeed, we are children of the King, for we have the promise that we are inheritors of that Kingdom. That promise is made valid by the seal of the indwelling Holy Spirit (Cf. Eph. 1:13, 14). And the Holy Spirit gives us the assurance that we will be able to pray as we ought. (Cf. Romans 8:26, 27). If so, then we are justified in using that phrase "in Jesus' Name," or "for Jesus' sake."

Experience persuades us that many prayers end with those words, but with no willful meaning, simply out of habit. Whenever they are used, it ought to indicate that even in our requests for material needs or physical blessings, our inmost desire is to *"seek first the kingdom of God and His righteousness ..."* (Matt. 6:33 NKJV).

When we petition God for help on the physical or human basis, it is logical that we ask "in Jesus' Name." What we are saying, in effect, is "Father, I have no right to come to you in my own name, but I come as your child, and as a disciple and servant of Jesus Christ, your Son. I claim that right, Father, because He has told us to come to You in His name. So, Father, I am bold to lift up to You my petition, and gladly acknowledge that I come only in the Name of my Lord and Savior, believing that You will hear and grant my request according to Your grace and wisdom."

Jesus is, indeed, the only way to God. His word stands firm and eternal, *"No one comes to the Father except through Me."* (John 14:6).

A Summary

To summarize the basic Scriptural meaning of the phrases, "in Jesus' name," and "for Jesus' sake," here is a brief statement:

1. "In Jesus' Name"

    1) I have no right to ask God for anything in my own name, but I am a believer in and servant of Christ, and He has told His disciples to ask in His name. So I am bold to ask for my needs, as He has taught us, believing He will hear and grant my request

    2) To ask for anything in Jesus' name should mean that what I pray for is, so far as I am able to judge, acceptable and pleasing to Him. Even when I ask for personal help, or in behalf of another, it should be something which, were He here on earth, I would have no hesitation in asking of Him. I should seek, so far as possible, to pray only for those things which Jesus approved when He was here on earth. To make petition in His name thus would mean I have thought through what I am asking, and feel

that it is some thing I would have no hesitancy in asking Him in person.

2. "For Jesus' sake

It is not only interesting but helpful to note some of the activities or attitudes brought into being because of devotion to Christ, or "for (His) sake." In Matt. 5:11, willing to be slandered or insulted (Cf. Luke 6:22); in Matt. 10:39, *". . he who has lost his life for My sake shall find it"*; in I Cor. 4:10, Paul says, *"We are fools for Christ's sake ..."*; in II Cor. 4:11, he says, *"For we who live are constantly being delivered over to death for Jesus' sake ..."*; and in II Cor. 12:10, the Apostle says, *". . I am well content with weaknesses, with insults, with distresses, with persecutions, with difficulties for Christ's sake. ."*; (Cf. Phil. 1:29; I Peter 2:13; III John 7).

From these it is easy to recognize that the only things which qualify "for Jesus' sake" are those which cost the believer something. He paid the supreme price for us. In return, if we do something to honor and glorify Him it must be something He would value. That means it must also be something of real value to us.

1) Whatever I ask is something that will honor and glorify Christ.

2) Whatever I ask for is for the purpose of extending or building up the Kingdom of God.

3) Whatever I ask is intended to be, according to my understanding, included in the will of God, and is submissive to His will, and I ask it because of the mission of our Lord, and thus for His sake.

4) No prayer for personal, or human needs, ought to be presented to God "for Jesus' sake." When we end a prayer with those words, it ought to be a prayer with one reason for its utterance – that which Jesus desires and for which He died – His mission on earth.

Fifteen

Staying with the Bible

PAUL WROTE TO TIMOTHY, *"All Scripture is inspired by God and profitable for teaching, for reproof, for correction, for training in righteousness; that the man of God may be adequate, equipped for every good work"* (2 Tim. 3:16, 17 NASB). The Bible is a book about God – God, the Father; His Son Jesus Christ; and the Holy Spirit of God. It is, at the same time, a book from God. He is the Author. It is a book in which we can find all we need to know about God and His love, and His wonderful, gracious plan for the redemption of sinful mankind. It is also a book which God uses to find us, in the sense of making us aware of His presence and His purposes, as we hear what He has to say to us in His Word. In this wonderful book, God gives us His wisdom in the plain instructions we find as to how to live, and how to discern the ways of God. It is a book which has much to say about 'prayer.'

It is the intention of the writer of this little book on 'prayer' that whatever is of any value in it will not be some attempt at human wisdom gathered from reputable sources, or distilled from human experience. It is an effort to cull from God's Word the teaching about 'prayer,' and the wisdom and instructions He gives. This is based on the conviction that no statement, or even testimony, about prayer has any validity unless it is based upon, or is in full agreement with, what God has given about 'prayer' in His Word. Prayer is not a device, or practice of men by which we are able to secure divine help. Rather, it is a gift of God by which He opens Himself to those who love Him, and want to be like Him, and who seek to know Him intimately. If there is any source from which truth about 'prayer' can be derived, it is the Bible. It is only in this Book that one can find ultimate truth about prayer and its practice. For only He who gave us 'prayer' as a wonderful privilege, can reveal its secrets.

It is important for us to be aware that the best preparation for prayer is a continuing, regular, diligent study of the Bible as the only authoritative source of information about prayer. In the Bible will be found all the purposes of prayer, all the right methods, with all the right motives, and all the characteristics of true prayer.

God never yells at us. His word to us is, *"Be still and know that I am God"* (Psalm 46:10). He uses many ways to communicate His truth to us, but it is when we are meditating upon His word that He is able to reach to the deepest recesses of our souls. It is in such moments that He most effectively plants His truth in our hearts and minds. There are times, of course, when God's Word comes to us like a fire, burning away the dross of our indolence, our complacency, our half-heartedness. And, on occasion, His word is like a hammer, shattering petty ideas, smashing vanity and pride, and destroying false concepts and notions. (Cf. Jeremiah 23:29). Most often He speaks to us in the quiet stillness of a moment when we have shut out everything else and have fastened our attention and thoughts on Him and His Word, seeking to know what He has to say to us.

Such attention and study is not prayer, but it is the best preparation one can make for effective praying. It is the height from which we can best see the limitless vastness of His majesty and might. It is there we can feel the healing, strengthening warmth of His love, and hear His tender voice giving us guidance and wisdom and power.

Jesus tells us, *"But you, when you pray, go into your inner room, and <u>when you have shut your door, pray ..."</u>* (Matt. 6:6 NASB). It is not always easy to shut the door so completely that no interference, or interruption, is possible. Our minds are so susceptible to extraneous and interfering thoughts. Attention to the Bible is one of the best ways to firmly shut the door to all outside duties, worries, or distractions. God will not seek to compete with any other voice. The door must be tightly shut, for He speaks to us as He did to Elijah, in *"a still, small voice"* (I Kings 19:12). When our efforts to pray are interrupted, and our prayer thoughts are pushed aside by petty ideas and a wandering mind, one of the best ways to push aside unwanted interventions is to recall and concentrate on familiar Bible truths and teachings.

Preparation for prayer is vital. There are times, of course, when in distress or great need, we simply cry out to God. And there are other times when our praying is spontaneous and without previous thought. There is good reason in such a moment to talk to God without waiting. God understands and honors those moments. But the times when we come closest to Him, and are more keenly aware of His presence, are more likely to be those when we have prepared our hearts and spirits to enter His throne room with humility and reverence. We cannot bring hatred, bitterness, pettiness, greed, jealousy, envy and other such attitudes into His presence. When they are present, God is far away. If we come with pride, vanity, selfishness, and their companions, we will not be permitted to enter where God is. We can wail our needs, but if our spirits are contaminated with evil characteristics of the flesh, God simply will not hear. His word to Judah, through Jeremiah, was *"for I do not hear you"* (7:16 NASB). Here again, the Bible is our best helper. The best way to rid ourselves of wrong attitudes, or a bad spirit, is simply to pick up God's Word and begin to read – the Holy Spirit will direct us to passages that cleanse our minds and prepare us to come to God in humility and purity.

The Bible has much to say about prayer, and gives us many examples of prayer. One of the best exercises for a Christian is to make a study of the prayers recorded in the Scriptures. We certainly would not want to imitate all of them, for in some there are dire imprecations invoked on enemies. Jesus forbade anything of that nature. (Cf. Mark 9:38-41). As disciples of Christ we know these are not in keeping with the love and forgiveness Jesus taught us to express in attitude and action. But by far the greater number are prayers we will do well to emulate.

There are a number of ways in which the Bible can be of help in our learning how to pray:

1. It is of utmost importance that we know something of God Himself. He gave us the privilege of prayer, and it is to Him we lift our petitions. The Bible provides for us the revelation of God in Christ – it is found nowhere else. Jesus said of Himself, *"He who has seen Me has seen the Father ..."* (John 14:9 NASB). Christ shows us the love and compassion, the holiness and righteousness, the wisdom and power of the Father. Because of His humanity He could not reveal the Father in totality, so we see only a part of the Divine landscape. But what we see is all that we, with the limitations of our humanity, can comprehend of the Almighty God. Yet through the incarnation – God in human flesh - and the revealed Scripture - we are privileged to grasp an awareness of the greatness and richness of God. But we are fully aware that God is outside and beyond and far greater than it all. And through the Scriptures we begin to see some of the facts about God which help us to pray. God moves, in a sense, on two levels – nature, and what we may call the supernatural. His outward actions are of two kinds, yet closely intertwined. There is, consequently, in our lives a polarity, a tension, for God works supernaturally in our human natures. By the Law, He teaches us to be honest, truthful, obedient to parents and those in authority, and in essence, to be decent human beings. At the same time, by the work of the Holy Spirit, we are to go far beyond that – to love even our enemies, and to be willing, if need be, to suffer for our faith. Jesus declared, *"If anyone wishes to come after Me, let him deny himself, and take up his cross, and follow Me."* (Matt. 16:24 NASB). God is at work in us, as it may seem, on two levels – we are to be the best that human nature can permit, but we are also to be a new order, a new creation – those who live by the Spirit. In our praying we must recognize that God is the source of all that is worthwhile humanly speaking, yet His greater blessing is that He lifts us above the ordinary, and helps us to know the

glory of the Kingdom of God. In our praying we will always find a tension, even a possible friction, between the desires of the flesh, and the eternal purposes of God. Familiarity with God's Word will help us to rise in our praying, from the mundane needs of our humanity, to the celestial opportunities of the Kingdom of God. God blesses us in that He enables us, by the power of the Spirit, to take care of human needs, but then to share with God Himself all the wonders of His grace and goodness as He brings His kingdom nearer to its fullness.

2. Human nature always seeks freedom – often expressed in rebellion against all authority, and disdain of the ways of God. But total freedom is found only in sinlessness – thus only God is free. Our sinful world has not the slightest idea of what that means. Jesus, as the sinless Son of Man, possessed that freedom. He could do whatever He wanted to do, because His desires were all within the concepts of Truth and Righteousness. These two are twin concepts and areas of ultimate reality. They are emanations of God's holiness. God possesses no desire for evil, no inclination toward it. He cannot be tempted, nor does He ever tempt His creatures. (Cf. James 1:13). But we are in bondage to sin, and capable of ever greater potential sinfulness. Without the salvation of Jesus Christ, every human being is totally captive to sin and unrighteousness. The wonder of the message of the Gospel is that God, who is pure and free, has sent His Son, Jesus, to be the Messiah, God incarnate, one of us, who lived a human life of total freedom. The holy God stoops to become one of us, subject to temptation even as we are, yet who lived without sin. And through our faith in Him, He comes to live in us so that we, too, can live without sin. We fall far short of our potential, to be sure, but in prayer we can look up to, and adore, our God who is able to make such a transformation in us, and out of sinful bondage bring freedom and holiness by His creative power. Knowledge of what God can do brings a transformation in our prayer life, so that even in our praying we have a freedom far beyond the understanding of mere human knowledge.

3. God is the ultimate, total, supreme good. This is part of the proposition of the Christian religion – from whatever viewpoint one may look – that the greatest good in life is to know God. Our prayer life is wonderfully enriched when we learn this truth, and thus seek in all the facets and circumstances of life to cultivate an awareness of God. The Bible is the greatest help in learning who God is, and the meaning of life in the light of God's love and grace. It guides us so that our praying can be oriented in the right direction, and for the right purposes. With its help we can pray in the will of God.

4. Because God is the supreme fact of the universe, in whom *"we live and move and exist"* (Acts 17:27 NASB), the most important thing we can ever do is to worship and adore Him. Adoration in prayer is more important than petition, or confession, or even thanksgiving. If we pay much attention to the Bible we cannot escape the truth confronting us that the ultimate purpose of prayer is to lead us to a full consciousness of God's holiness, love and grace. An almost automatic word will be "How great Thou art!"

5. A thorough study of the Bible will also help us to see the tremendous difference between some of the prayers of the Old Testament, particularly in the Psalms, to those of the New Testament, climaxing with Jesus' own prayers. Such a study will reveal the difference between the prayers of David calling down destruction on his enemies, and that of the New Testament wherein there is earnest petition for spiritual growth and blessings, enabling the committed Christian to obey in sincerely praying even for those who count themselves as our enemies.

In the final analysis, the knowledge which enables us to pray most effectively is not a science, in which we learn the 'Do's' and 'Don't's'. Rather, it is to know God intimately, and for that, the Bible is imperative, indeed indispensable.

6. The Bible also helps us to know the place our humanity plays in God's eternal plan and purpose. For it is only when we know who we are, and the relationship we have with God, that prayer will

have its proper place in our lives. We are born in sin, and regardless of our morals, we are sinful creatures, separated from God until, by His grace, He brings us to repentance, confession and faith in Christ. As a Christian, a child of God, the Bible becomes the most valuable single possession. For it is only in the Bible that we can find the truth which enables us to know God in Christ, and to know ourselves. And it is there that we are given instructions as to how to pray, what to pray for, and the place of prayer in our participation in the kingdom of God.

Sixteen

Continue in Persistence

JESUS HAS TAUGHT US to pray persistently. That does not mean we are to bombard heaven's doors until somebody responds. It does mean we are to continue to express our faith that God will hear and answer if what we are asking is worthy of His consideration. Such praying is an expression of our trust in the wisdom and mercy of God. If we are led of the Spirit, God will help us to know if what we are asking is unworthy, or contrary to His will, so that we will not waste our time.

There are those who say that if you have enough faith, you should ask God only once for whatever it is you desire, then claim it on the basis of your faith, and leave the request in His hands. But Jesus clearly taught there are times when persistence in praying is desirable, even essential. In two parables Jesus gave us instruction (Luke 11:5-10; 18:1-8). In the first lesson, Jesus has just finished giving the disciples the Model Prayer. He continues with the parable of one going to friend at night asking for three loaves to feed an unexpected visitor. His lesson was, *"I tell you, even though he will not get up and give him anything because he is his friend, <u>yet because of his persistence he will get up and give him as much as he needs."</u>* The second lesson begins <u>*"Now He was telling them a parable to show that at all times they ought to pray and not*</u>

lose heart." Then continues the parable of the widow who continued to come to the judge for help. The punch line here is *". .now shall not God bring about justice for His elect, who cry to Him day and night, and will he delay long over them? I tell you, He will bring about justice for them speedily."* In these two lessons Jesus is teaching with great emphasis that we ought always pray and not faint. God does not regard our persistence as a nuisance.

In the first parable, the lesson is a bit startling. In verse 8, the word we translate "importunity," or "persistence," has a basic meaning of "shamelessness." The man who has a need comes knocking on the door of his neighbor and friend in the middle of the night, asking for help – three loaves of bread. Of all things – bread, the simplest thing – and of all times, in the middle of the night. The friend says, "Don't bother me at this time of night. We are all in bed." But the man in need is "SHAMELESS;" he continues to persist until finally the friend rises and gives him what he needs.

Jesus is surely telling us that God wants us to draw near to Him with the realization that we have needs which only He can supply. There is nowhere else for us to go. The man knocking on his neighbor's door was not asking anything for himself. He had a genuine need, but it was not for himself. His 'shamelessness' was impelled by that need. The Psalmist assures us, *"the eyes of the Lord are toward the righteous, and His ears are open to their cry ... .The righteous cry and the Lord hears, and delivers them out of all their troubles"* (Ps. 34:15, 17 NASB).

When the Syro-Phoenician woman came asking Jesus for help for her daughter who was demon-possessed, He seemed almost rude in His response to her plea. But she was "shameless" in her pleading for His help. The result was that Jesus said to her *"O woman, your faith is great; be it done for you as you wish"* (Matt. 15:28 NASB).

Any thinking person will know there are some things God will not grant because they are contrary to His will. Occasionally, when our wills are arrayed against His will, He will permit us to have what we seem determined to have. The Scripture tells us of occasions when God gave the Israelites what they wanted, even though it was not His will for them. It was part of His judgment upon them. It happened in their trek through the wilderness, when they complained about the manna. God told them they would have meat *"until it come out of your nostrils and becomes loathsome to you"* (Numbers 11:20 NASB). The Psalmist says of this, *"And he gave them their request: but sent leanness into their souls (a wasting disease among them)"* (106:15). Later, when Israel wanted a king, God told Samuel, *"Listen to the voice of the people … for they have not rejected you, but they have rejected Me from being king over them"* (I Sam. 8:7 NASB). In such instances, God does not run roughshod over our wills, but His purpose in permitting us to have what we may seem determined to have is to teach us a lesson, and at the same time let His judgment leave its mark on us. If we yield to the leading of the Holy Spirit, we will never persist in this measure. For the Spirit will give us the knowledge and the wisdom to distinguish between what we NEED to pray for, and the things we might want merely for selfish purposes.

God is not irked by our persistence in prayer. His word plainly tells us, *"Ask, and it shall be given to you; seek, and you shall find; knock, and it shall be opened to you"* (Matt. 7:7 NASB). He is not reluctant to give us what is good. Indeed, just the opposite is true. But, with His great knowledge and wisdom, and acting always in perfect love, He knows that often there are other blessings of more importance in our spiritual lives than the immediate answer to our prayers. God's timing is perfect. So, if He does not give us quickly what we ask, it is because He has something better in store for us. He knows what our real need is, and that what we are asking is not of immediate importance.

Christians need to learn that God's purpose in our lives is not to make us happy with things, or to satisfy our wants, but rather to assist us in becoming adults mature in the faith. There is always such danger of our being attracted by the outward appearance of things. If He gave us everything we ask for when we wanted it, we would remain "babes in Christ," childish in our attitudes and desires. It is spiritually infantile to ask only for the material and physical blessings. God wants us to grow up to the stage that our cry will be for the Holy Spirit in power with the spiritual blessings He provides.

God uses our persistence in prayer to help us sort out our requests so that we soon learn to ask for those things that have eternal values. We will have learned the lesson Jesus wanted to teach – if we are persistent in prayer for the real needs of our lives, God hears our pleas. When there are personal needs which only God can provide, He does not rebuke us when we persist in our petitions. As with Paul, when he asked three times that his 'thorn in the flesh' might be removed, God may not grant the request, but He always answers. With Paul, He promised that His grace would be sufficient to enable him to bear that 'thorn in the flesh' gracefully and with profit. We can be sure that God never turns a deaf ear to our pleading for help. Whatever His answer may be, it will be a blessing helpful to us and useful in the Kingdom of God.

We can believe that one of God's purposes in waiting to grant our requests is to help us become strong in our prayer life by urging us to pray hard for those things we know are important, and perhaps even essential. When a strong person sets out to do something, he or she does not stop if the first efforts seem failures. It is said that when someone upbraided Thomas Edison for thousands of efforts to create the incandescent light bulb as 'wasted', that his reply was in essence, "Oh no! Those are ways we know will not work." The persistent person keeps working until the objective is accomplished. Even so, the person who is strong in prayer does not wilt if the answer is not immediately forthcoming. That persistence is not the result of personal will-power, but rather, is based on an abiding faith in the love, goodness, grace, wisdom and mercy of God.

While I was in the seminary, another student and I were assigned as a lesson project to interview one of the older pastors in the city as to his way of handling the pastorate – his habits, practices and procedures, etc. In the interview he revealed that he kept a long prayer list. He picked it up from his desk and pointed to two names, saying, "I have been praying for those two men for forty years. I still have faith that God will save them."

One may ask, "If God wants a person to be saved, why should it take forty years or more of praying to bring about a person's salvation?" This is one of the mysteries of our faith, but it is logical to say two things: First, is that God has His own time table, and there is a divine reason for it; second, it is logical to say that God never forces Himself on anyone. He will not compel a person to believe. Faith is a gift which must be received gladly. Meanwhile, the Holy Spirit continues to work in quietness and love to woo a lost person to the love and grace of God. One thing we do know is that God does answer prayers which are persistent for many years, and we can be thankful for that.

God wants us to have all that is good. It is growth in knowledge and wisdom which enables us to distinguish what is good in God's sight, and what is merely humanly desirable. If there is something which is useful and needed in the Kingdom of God, then it is our privilege and responsibility to pray for it. And we must keep praying, for God yearns to give what is good, and He will give it when the time is right.

If what I ask is something that seems good to me, but I do not have witness of the Spirit that it is good in God's sight, I am foolish to persist. But if what I ask is something I desperately need, and only God can give it; or if it is something I am sure is in accordance with God's purposes and plans, then I should have no difficulty in persisting as long as I am willing to wait for God to answer. None of us will ever reach the stage where every prayer is answered just as we want it to be. In that case God would be just a servant doing our bidding. But the earnest, spiritually minded person will become more and more in tune with God, and thus more and more sensitive to the will and purposes of God. God promises to hear and answer when we pray within His will.

John tells us of Lazarus' illness and death. Jesus, at that time, was on the other side of the Jordan River, at the place where John first baptized. When Lazarus became ill, the sisters immediately sent for Jesus, saying "Lord, behold, he whom You love is sick." It was a prayer for His help. We can be sure that if they had had ways to convey that message, they would have sent it every day. But when Jesus received that word, His answer for the benefit of the disciples who were with Him, was *"This sickness is not unto death, but for the glory of God, that the Son of God may be glorified by it."* (John 11:4 NASB.) John is careful to tell us that Jesus "loved Martha, and her sister, and Lazarus." So one might wonder, Why in the world did He not hurry to their side? But John further tells us *"When therefore He heard that he was sick, He stayed then two days longer in the place where He was."* (11:6). There is surely no question as to whether Jesus could have healed Lazarus if He had gone to his side quickly. In fact, we are sure that had He wanted to do so, He could have healed him from a distance. He did just that in other instances (Cf. Matt. 8:5-13). And it is not likely that He would have hurried had the sisters sent several messages pleading with Him to come to their aid. The reason – " .*that the Son of God may be glorified by it.*" This is simply a reminder that God has His own time-table. But if when a child of God prays for help of some sort, and there is no immediate answer from God, to cease praying is a sign of faithlessness. Jesus would say firmly, "Keep on praying."

Seventeen

Depending on the Holy Spirit

IT SEEMS EVIDENT THAT the power of the Holy Spirit is sadly lacking in the churches across Europe and North America. The past generation violated the moral codes – they committed adultery, they lied, stole, and developed a spirit of gambling, bribery and deceit. But they recognized those moral codes as legitimate and even desirable. However, today's generation repudiates the very moral codes themselves. Homosexuals say their life-style is as good as any, and in many instances the churches are saying the same thing – we must not in any way differentiate between the gays and others. The current status of morality is that nothing is inherently right or wrong: situational ethics has taken over. Society as a whole is saying that every individual has the right to say what is right or wrong for himself or herself. Morality is purely a personal matter.

In this kind of society, the talk is of social values. The news media blazons to the world that the problem is not morality. Meanwhile, the churches by and large attack the problem with bandaids. There is little straightforward preaching and teaching of God's Word. The humanism of the world has invaded the churches and much of the effort is to provide fellowship and fun, counseling without constraint, and inspiration without truth.

What is it that a person who has a deep, anguished concern for the situation can do? Pray. Surely in the heart of every true Christian is the yearning that there might be a change for the better in our society. Is not your heart heavy as you see all the mounting evil around us? Is there any hope for change? Instinctively, we know there is no power that can change one person, much less an evil world, except God. And we also know there is only one way His power can be brought into play in our world, and that is through the Gospel of Jesus Christ. We fully recognize the truth in Peter's words, *"And there is salvation in no one else; for there is no other name under heaven that has been given among men, by which we must be saved"* (Acts 4:12 NASB). It is so important to remember that praying is the most spiritual activity in which a person can engage. There can be no hypocrisy, no impure desires or thoughts, no unworthy motives in the mind and heart of the person who seeks contact with our Almighty God. The use of religious words may sound soothing and attractive, but may accomplish nothing, if the spirit is not right.

It may sound strange, but in its simplest meaning prayer has to do with conflict. We are talking about conflict in the spiritual realm. There is a war going on. The object of the conflict is to determine who will control the earth and its inhabitants. Jesus Christ is the rightful Prince of the realm, but Satan is doing all in his power to dethrone the Prince; he is the pretender, having been thrown out of heaven. But he is doing all in his power to control the populace and oust the rightful ruler. This is a spiritual conflict. Man is a spirit-being embodied in flesh. So the conflict involves all the human beings on earth. It is of a spirit-nature, in the spirit-realm, involving spirit-beings. That means we are in the midst of it, on one side or the other. Satan is the head of the enemy army, seeking with cunning and deceit to secure consent of the spirits and bodies of human beings. If he cannot secure our participation on his side, he will do all he can to disarm and disorient us so that we are ineffective soldiers on the Lord's side. The only power which is effective in this war is moral, spiritual power. God does not use force with men and women. Satan, however, works to convince people that the physical and the material are all important and all-powerful. Many Christians are misled into thinking that the battle will be won with human and material resources.

Because this is a spirit conflict, the greatest weapon in the arsenal of our King and His army is 'prayer.' In essence, this is the insistent claiming by the soldiers of the King that the same power by which our Lord Jesus Christ defeated Satan in the 'temptations' shall be extended to the lives of those who now oppose Christ by bringing them under conviction of the Spirit, and hopefully to salvation, while at the same time giving those already in the army of the Lord the moral and spiritual power of the Lord as they face the evil which confronts them. The marvel of the weapon of 'prayer' is that it has no limitations. Only a few can go as missionaries to far places, but the range of prayer has no boundary lines.

The Christian has two offensive weapons – the Word of God and prayer. Paul tells us, *"With all prayer and petition pray at all times in t he Spirit ..."* (Eph. 6:18 NASB). In the lines immediately preceding the above, he gives us a list of the defensive armor we have, but he winds up declaring *".. and take ... .the sword of the Spirit, which is the word of God."* (Eph. 6:17b NASB). The defensive armor is vital, but the battle will not be won if the soldiers of the Lord sit down and passively depend on their armor to protect them. The battle must be taken to the enemy, and our two offensive weapons must be wisely and vigorously used to defeat him. Prayer is like having a bow with many arrows. As an arrow must be aimed at a specific target to have any value, so our prayers must be definite, specific, and persistent.

Praying for a victory in a universe-wide war may seem like painting an acre-wide picture with a one-eighth inch brush. We have to confess that we do not know how to pray as we should. But it is glorious to realize that God knows we have need of help, so He has provided that help. He helps where the petition is made, in the one who prays, and where it is delivered, in the object of the prayer. The Holy Spirit, who is the guaranty of our redemption, and God's seal in us who are saved, is also our Helper in prayer. At the same time, our Lord Jesus

Himself is our Advocate in the presence of the Father. What more could we ask? With the Holy Spirit here, and the Lord Jesus there, we have the bases covered. Note how God takes care of our situation.

All true prayer is called for by the leading of the Holy Spirit. There will be no genuine approach to God except by the motivation and direction of the Spirit. The Holy Spirit produces in us that state of mind which is essential for prayer. Prayer is first of all an expression of our wants and desires, a pouring out before God of what we would like to see become realities. It is also a recognition of our utter poverty, for we can bring nothing into God's presence except our total emptiness. He will do nothing for us or with us as long as we come to Him holding fast what we regard as our own resources. A great example is the account of Gideon and the defeat of the Midianites. Gideon was called into service by an angel, and the Lord assured him saying, *"Surely I will be with you, and you shall defeat Midian as one man."* (Judges 6:16 NASB). So Gideon started out with 32,000 soldiers, but God said to him, *"The people who are with you are too many for Me to give Midian into their hands, lest Israel become boastful ..."* (7:2). Then 22,000 went home, but the Lord again said, *"The people are still too many ..."* (7:4). So Gideon wound up with only 300 soldiers to face an enemy *"lying in the valley as numerous as locusts"* (7:12). Then the amazing fact is that those 300 men were each armed only with a trumpet and an empty pitcher with a torch inside. No sword or javelin, not even a shield, but the victory was theirs. How did that come about? God did it all. Their only part was trust and obedience.

One other thing was needed. They had to recognize their complete dependence on God. That is equally true with us. With David we can say, *"My soul waits in silence for God only; from Him is my salvation. ... This poor man cried and the Lord heard him ... .* (Ps. 62:1; 34:6 NASB).

By the gift of the Spirit, we have a new nature which is able to look up and aspire to the things of God, because that new life in us is from God. When in conscious weakness, dependence and need that new nature reaches out to the Father in love, and with humble petition, that cry is heard by Him in whom dwells love in all its fullness. God the Father and the creature made in His image meet together and blend in an act of holy fellowship. God welcomes His child into His presence, and faith is rewarded according to the Father's love and wisdom. Prayer gets no farther than the ceiling unless it begins with the full recognition that we are helpless, and our only resource is our loving God.

<u>The Spirit helps us to prepare ourselves for prayer.</u> God has promised to hear us, but one does not enter the presence of the Almighty God without proper preparation. True, Jesus said, *"Knock, and it shall be opened unto you"* (Matt. 7:7). But we must come with humility and in the beauty of holiness, with sins confessed and forgiven. And we must approach the throne of God with reverence. When the prophet Isaiah had his vision of God, his instant reaction was the realization of his sinfulness, revealed in his words, *"Woe is me ... for I am a man of unclean lips ..."* (Isa. 6:5 NASB). When we are serious in seeking to talk to God, we quickly learn that just speaking words into space is no more than hearing our own voices. To have the consciousness that God is really listening to us, it takes moments of silence as we turn our minds from the mundane affairs of life and bring our thoughts in an upturned attitude concentrating on the One whom we seek. It is here that the Holy Spirit is our Helper. It is He who brings us into the presence of God. He is God. When He is resident in us, then our spirits can be in tune with Him, and communication is possible. It is important that we become actively obedient to the Spirit, not just passively resigned to the will of God as a force we cannot evade. To be in tune with God means we desire what He desires. The Holy Spirit works in our hearts, minds, lives to help us sincerely desire to do the will of God. Thus He prepares us for prayer.

<u>The Holy Spirit is our teacher helping us know how to pray.</u> Paul reminds us that we do not know how to pray as we ought. (Cf. Rom. 8:26). The more we pray the more aware we become of our need at this point. The entreaty of the fervent heart is that of the disciples, "Lord, teach us to pray." Jesus promised, *"But the Helper, the Holy Spirit, whom the Father will send in My Name, He will teach you all things ..."* (John 14:26 NASB). Chief in the curriculum of the Spirit is 'prayer.' It is all important in the spiritual war in which we are part of the battlefield,

as well as soldiers in the battle. Praying in the Spirit means willingness to wait on the Spirit to give us guidance – not running ahead of God. It also means having an outlook of expectancy – anticipating what God in His lovingkindness provides for our needs. At a Prayer Breakfast, an elderly saint of God, who was asked to begin the prayer period, hesitated for a moment, then began, "Father, you have given us so much, we do not know what we should ask for, so just give us some more of your wonderful surprises today."

The Spirit also helps us with regard to our desires. Prayer must begin with something we want and desire earnestly, but it has to be accompanied with the awareness of our utter poverty, and the acknowledgment of our total dependence. We have nothing with which to start except emptiness. The wants and desires of the worldling who does not know God are on the opposite end from the plans and purposes of God. But the Christian can start from the right place because we have been given the Spirit of God Himself to instruct us and guide us and help us to pray. God is solicitous for His children. It is the loving care of an attentive Father for those who belong to him. He wants the best for them. But when we start in the Christian life, it is not easy for us to turn completely away from worldly desires to spiritual concerns. But this is part of the blessed work of the Holy Spirit – to help us know what it is that God wants, not just OF us, but also FOR us. As we study God's Word, and as we grow in our prayer life, our interest in and concern for God's Kingdom increases, and our desires grow more and more into line with God's will. The Holy Spirit then teaches us the things for which we ought to pray.

Praying in the Spirit also means eagerness to know what it is that God has in store for us - listening to hear God's instructions and commands, and being prepared to respond. The Holy Spirit is our Helper. The Name "Comforter" is often used to denote the Spirit, but the name "Helper" is a better designation of His ministry. It is hard for us to understand, but God's Word assures us that the Holy Spirit *"Himself intercedes for us with groanings too deep for words"* (Rom. 8:26 NASB). A loving mother fully understands the cry of her baby – no words are spoken; none are needed. She recognizes the variations, and the meanings of them, in that cry. And if that baby is sick, or hurt, or having real problems of any sort, the Mother will respond with inner groanings of compassion, and a personal desire to do whatever she can to minister to the needs of her child. Even so, God, by His Spirit, understands the unuttered longings and desires of our hearts, especially our spiritual yearnings, and He wills to have us help which only He can give. The Spirit will reveal to us our true needs, and help us to ask for what is good in God's sight. The wonder is that He goes beyond that in pleading our case, even as we lift our prayers to God. His thoughts may find no verbal response in us – our lips cannot express the Spirit's impressions because we have not matured to the point that we can verbalize His concepts. But if our own spirits are in tune with God's purposes and desires, then the Spirit communicates with the Father – the heart-searcher that He is – and He knows fully what the Spirit is saying within us.

<u>The Holy Spirit will also give us boldness in our praying.</u> John tells us, *"And this is the confidence which we have before Him, that, if we ask anything according to His will, He hears us. And if we know that He hears us in whatever we ask, we know that we have the requests which we have asked from Him"* (I John 5:14, 15 NASB) The writer of Hebrews urges , *"Let us therefore draw near with confidence to the throne of grace, that we may receive mercy and may find grace to help in time of need."* And later he adds, *". . so that we confidently say, THE LORD IS MY HELPER, I WILL NOT BE AFRAID"* (Heb. 4:16; 13:6 NASB). If God wants something, and I want the same thing, then God's Word assures me that if I ask for it, the prayer will be granted. The Holy Spirit gives me the assurance in my heart that I am in the will of God, and that my request is something God wants to give. So I pray with confidence. It is important, therefore, that we work at the job of bringing our desires into the frame-work of God's desires. His Word will provide the needed information, and the Holy Spirit will affirm it as a fact. So, to ask for those things that I know are not in the will of God is to work directly against Almighty God – what foolishness!

<u>All that the Spirit does for us as God's children is summed up in the wonderful truth that we *'have received a spirit of adoption as sons by</u>*

which we cry out, "Abba, Father," (Rom. 8:15 NASB). Through the Word and the guidance of the Holy Spirit we know that in prayer we are not addressing a stern, forbidding Person who keeps Himself sufficiently separated from those who approach Him, but a loving Father who holds out to us welcoming arms. He endows us with the Holy Spirit as His seal of ownership, and by the Spirit we are sanctified in truth, thus purified and permitted to come into the presence of our God, and know that our prayers are heard and answered.

To sum up the importance of the Holy Spirit in helping us to be truly prayer warriors, here is what He does: He helps us prepare our own spirits for prayer. He helps us know what we should pray for. He gives us boldness in approaching our Heavenly Father. He works constantly to teach us what true prayer is and how to pray. And when all is said and done, when we do not know how to pray as we should, He even takes our place, and intercedes for us, putting into the hand of the Father what we should be asking. No words are necessary. The Father knows what the mind of the Spirit is, because the Spirit works only according to the will of God.

To be helped by the Spirit, there must be no opposition to Him or differing from the known will of God. If He is to direct, or help us with our prayers, we cannot be in conflict with Him. The Word of God assures us that if we pray in the Spirit, God moves freely to grant our requests. Satan's world of power, pleasures, pride and material things will grow smaller, and of decreasing importance to us, while the things of Christ will fill the horizons of our lives. The Holy Spirit will stimulate us to holy endeavor.

Eighteen

Sharing in the Kingdom of God

Humanism has its Christian counterpart – the concept that God's real concern and interest is in helping His children with their needs. A sad fact is that much of the Christianity of today is a general welfare program based on the belief that to serve God is a matter of doing good..

The Washington National cathedral is a beautiful building, and we can hope that it serves a needed and worthy purpose. But a statement by the Dean of the Cathedral as to the purpose of the institution reminds us of how humanistic the basic religion of America has become. His statement was as follows:

> "As your National House of Prayer for All People, the Washington National Cathedral seeks to be: 'A voice of generous-spirited Christianity; a place of reconciliation; a people committed to ministering with compassion to the needs of our world'"

Change the word 'Christianity' to that of some other organization, and it could be a worthy statement for any benevolent effort. And the sad fact is that the above statement would satisfy a large percentage of our churches. The dominant aim of most of them is to help one another and others. The greater portion of what most of the churches do has little to do with the Kingdom of God. There seems to be very little emphasis on the extension of God's Kingdom. What about the exaltation of our Lord Jesus Christ? The Dean of the Cathedral, and many others, would probably say, "Well, yes; we hope those take place." But they are, in reality, for the Cathedral and many other churches, just "Add-ons." And the tragic truth is that unless they are our priorities, they will not take place at all.

No one would argue against our ministering to the needs of people. But is that the highest objective of our prayer life? When we look at Paul's prayers, two basic desires shine through. First, when he asks others to pray for him, very little that is physical or material is there. It is largely that he may be faithful in preaching the gospel. In his letter we call "Ephesians" he says, *"pray on my behalf that utterance may be given me in the opening of my mouth to make known with boldness the mystery of the gospel ... .that in proclaiming it I may speak boldly, as I ought to speak"* (Eph 6:19, 20 NASB). (Cf. Phil. 2:19,20; Col. 4:3) And in his prayers for others, he voices primarily his earnest desire for their spiritual growth and faithfulness to God's kingdom. (Cf. Eph. 1: 15-19a; 3:14-19; Phil. 1:9-11; Col. 1:9-11).

If our prayer life is to fit into God's plans and purposes, then we cannot ignore the fact that God's priority is His Kingdom, not our wellbeing. One tiny little phrase ought to help us see where our personal priorities should be. Anybody ought to be willing to give another person a drink of water, if needed. What's so special about that? Nothing, if it is just a human kindness. But Jesus said, *"I tell you the truth, anyone who gives you a cup of water in My name because you belong to Christ, will certainly not lose his reward"* (Mark 9:41 NIV). Jesus is saying that if one of His disciples receives even a cup of water, given in His name, solely because he or she is a disciple, the one who gives the water will NOT lose the reward. There must be something more to this matter of being a follower of Christ than being just a kind-hearted passerby. We have noted more than once Jesus' command, *"Seek first the kingdom of God ... "* Evidently, Jesus meant what He said – the kingdom of God is to be first in our concerns and objectives.

When Jesus taught His disciples about prayer, it is very important to see what His emphases were and are. After the address, *"Our Father, Who art in heaven"*, the first phrase is *"Hallowed be Thy name."* That is both a declaration of worship, and a petition. The next words are *"Thy kingdom come, Thy will be done on earth as it is in heaven."* There is where our priority in life must be. It is not to be just a kind, attentive neighbor. Our first responsibility as a follower of Jesus Christ is to *"seek first His kingdom and His righteousness."* (Matt. 6:33). Jesus said, *"I must preach the good news of the kingdom of God .... because that is why I was sent"* (Luke 4:43). In the Sermon on the Mount, virtually all that Jesus taught deals with citizenship in the kingdom of God. He sums it up by saying, *"You cannot serve both God and mammon."* There are only two ways of living – for God or for the world.

All that we do in benefit of others counts in God's plan only if done in the Name of Jesus Christ. Good deeds such as giving a cup of water to a thirsty person should be normal for every person. But as Christians, our objective when we minister to others, is that those good deeds are done not in order to enter the kingdom of God, but because we ARE already children of God and citizens of His kingdom. The good deeds that help others are to be simply the overflow of a life committed to worshipping and serving God, exalting the name of Jesus Christ, and being obedient to the Holy Spirit. The life emphasis of the true believer in Jesus Christ is to extend His kingdom. To focus primarily on helping other human beings, without regard for our representation of Jesus Christ as our Lord, is to be humanistic, or even secularistic. The emphasis of all we do should be to bring glory to God. And that covers our prayer life also.

God's Word clearly indicates that the greatest work a person can do is to seek in every way possible to bring the Kingdom of God nearer to its consummation. Nothing else is of importance in comparison. Daniel records words given him in revelation: *"Then the sovereignty, the dominion, and the greatness of all the kingdoms under the whole heaven will be given to the people of the saints of the Highest One; His kingdom will be an everlasting kingdom, and all the dominions will serve and obey Him"* (Dan. 7:27 NASB).

Our greatest respsonsibility, and indeed, our greatest privilege, is to share in the kingdom of our God. How does that affect our prayers, and our prayer life? It simply means that the primary objective of all our praying must be God's kingdom. When we consider the fact that God has given us the wonderful privilege of sharing not only in the extension of His kingdom, but that He has adopted us into His family and thus has made us "heirs of God and fellow heirs with Christ," then there should be no question as to what our priority in praying should be. When this kingdom is one we will share in the inheritance, surely our prayer life should be and will be focused on building that kingdom, with special emphasis on our own participation in all its opportunities and resultant blessings.

Did it ever occur to you that God's first commitment is to His own glory? At first glance, it may seem strange, but everything God does is for His own glory. If that be true, then obviously all we do should have the same purpose. We should never forget that the most God-centered Person in the universe is God Himself. Jesus began His prayer in John 17 saying, *"Father ... . glorify Your Son that Your Son may glorify You ... . I have glorified You on earth ... . And now, O Father, glorify Me together with Yourself, with the glory which I had with You before the world was. ."* (John 17:1, 4 5). We ask, "What is the chief end of man?" The answer is "To glorify God and enjoy Him forever." If we ask "What is the chief end of God?" then the answer has to be, "To glorify Himself and enjoy His glory forever."

Does that shake you up a bit? We are so accustomed to thinking of God in terms of what He can and will do for us, that we fail to grasp the fact that His glory is the aim of all creation, and thus His basic purpose in all He does.

Many people consider themselves to be God-centered as long as they feel that God is man-centered. It is easy to think of God as the center of our universe as long as He is the means for our self-esteem and self-satisfaction. Humanism is a very subtle and dangerous thing. It may be hard to say, but God loves His glory more than He loves us, and, in fact, that is the foundation of His love for us. Isaiah reminds us, *"All the nations are as nothing before Him, they are regarded by Him as less than nothing and meaningless"* (40:17 NASB). God's full commitment is to Himself, not to us. Do you find that hard to accept? Let God Himself speak. He says, *"For the sake of My Name I delay My wrath, and for My praise I restrain it for you in order not to cut you off .... For MY own sake, for My own sake, I will act .... and My glory I will not give to another."* (Isa. 48:9, 11).

Ezekiel also reminds us, *"It is not for your sake, O house of Israel, that I am about to act, but for MY holy Name ...."* (36:22).

Salvation is a wonderful gift of God to us human beings. But that salvation is for the purpose of bringing glory to Himself. He desires that we shall come to know Him as our God, and then offer up to Him our adoration, worship, praise and thanksgiving. For the only real glory God gets from His creation is from us who are made in His image, and have the power of our wills to glorify Him in all we do. We should ever keep all this in mind as we pray. Even when we pray for our personal needs, or in behalf of someone else, God, apparently, will hear our prayers only if the motivation for our lives is the kingdom of our Lord. God's purpose in sending His Son Jesus Christ to give us salvation is that His kingdom might be expanded, and thus that He might receive glory from, in and through us as His adopted children.

The dynamic for all our prayer life should be that God's will may be done in and through us, remembering that the final word is, *". . . that at the name of Jesus every knee should bow .... and that every tongue should confess that Jesus Christ is Lord, to the GLORY OF GOD THE FATHER."* (Phil. 2:10,11 NASB)

If our objective in working and praying is the Kingdom of God, just what does that cover ? It seems obvious that it begins with the desire for God to be glorified and worshipped everywhere and by all His creation. David, the Psalmist, voiced it long ago, *"O Lord, our Lord, how majestic is Thy name in all the earth, who hast displayed Thy splendor above the heavens ..."* (Ps. 8:1 NASB). Today. Christians around the world sing "How Great Thou Art!" All beautiful words. No matter how it may be phrased, such a prayer finds it real meaning only in the spirit and intention of the one who voices the words. This is where one's concern for the Kingdom of God begins -- to pray that

His Kingdom will come in all its fullness. But again we are mindful that words by themselves can be empty. It is the spirit behind them that makes them real.

The point of all this is that if our prayers have no relationship to God and His will, and His Kingdom, He will have little reason to pay attention. But if we are obeying Jesus Christ's commandment to *"Seek first the kingdom of God and His rightgeousness"* then He will have an interest in all our needs, desires, efforts, and intentions. Our relationship to God – Father, Son and Holy Spirit – is the determining factor in the effectiveness of our prayers.

To put it bluntly – God's evaluation of our prayers depends on our evaluation of Him and His kingdom. If we are in tune with Him, then He will be willing to get in tune with us. But if our concern is primarily for ourselves – our needs, our problems, our objectives, our desires, without much regard for His eternal plans and purposes – then He, according to what we can glean from the Holy Scriptures, will not have much in- terest or regard for our objectives. He will, in essence, be saying to us, "If you are going to go your way, then you will go alone – I won't be there. But go My way, and I will never leave you nor forsake you."

The Kingdom of God is not of this world. Jesus plainly said, *"My kingdom is not of this world. If My kingdom were of this world, then My servants would be fighting, that I might not be delivered up to the Jews; but as it is, My kingdom is not of this realm"* (John 18:36 NASB). Yet Jesus bluntly told the disciples *"But seek first His kingdom and His righteousness; and all these things shall be added to you"* (Matt. 6:33 NASB). He has also taught us to pray *"Thy kingdom come. Thy will be done on earth as it is in heaven"* (Matt. 6:10 NASB).

The Pharisees of Jesus' day thought of the kingdom in terms of the day when Israel would be restored to its former greatness; so they asked Jesus, then at the height of His popularity, "When is the kingdom of God coming?" They were thinking in terms of signs and outward evidences. Jesus quickly replied, *"The kingdom is not coming with signs to be observed; nor will they say 'Look, here it is!' or 'There it is!' For behold the kingdom of God is in your midst"* (Lk. 17:20, 21 NASB).

Jesus was clearly implying that the kingdom is not in outward signs – churches, schools, and the like. It is certainly not observed in advancing prosperity, nor scientific progress. Paul tells us, *"The kingdom of God is not eating and drinking, but righteousness and peace and joy in the Holy Spirit"* (Romans 14:17 NASB). The Kingdom is a spiritual realm. A hard fact to realize is that the kingdom is in those who know, love and worship God. God rules and works <u>in</u> us, as well as by and through us.

The Bible tells us all we know about the kingdom of God, or Heaven, as it is also called. <u>First, it is a present reality and power.</u> Mark records, *"Jesus came into Galilee, preaching the gospel of God, and saying, 'The time is fulfilled, and the kingdom of God is at hand'"* (Mark 1:14, 15 NASB). Paul wrote to Timothy, *"Jesus Christ . . . . who is the blessed and only Sovereign, the King of kings, and Lord of lords"* (I Tim. 6:14, 15 NASB). Much of the New Testament would be meaningless without the fact that Jesus Christ is truly King of kings and Lord of lords. He assured the disciples, *"All authority is given unto Me in heaven and on earth"* (Matt. 28:18). He did not use the Greek word generally translated "power', but a stronger word which means the full authority to exercise power and command. He gave full evidence of that authority in multiply-ing the loaves and fishes, in stilling the storm, in healing the sick and suffering, in bringing the dead to life, in dozens of other ways, and in rising from the dead. He is the King of that kingdom which continues to spread its reach, and one day will be the only government there is.

<u>Second, it is an eternal kingdom.</u> The prophet Isaiah declared, *"There will be no end to the increase of His government, or of peace, on the throne of David and over His kingdom, to establish it and to uphold it with justice and righteousness from then on and forevermore"* (Isa. 9:7 NASB). Paul affirms that *at the name of Jesus every knee should bow of those who are in heaven, and on earth, and under the earth, and that every tongue should confess that Jesus Christ is Lord, to the glory of God the Father"* (Phil. 2:10, 11 NASB).

One of the greatest privileges we have as those redeemed from sin and saved by the grace of God is that of praying for the coming of this kingdom. We can pray for the coming of that kingdom in our own lives, to the end that we are doing the will of God. We can pray that our homes will give every evidence of being part of that kingdom, showing forth in every way possible the characteristics of the King Himself. We can pray that our church will be more than an institution, but will be truly the body of Christ in this place where we live We can pray that the kingdom will come in our community, demonstrated by obedience to the laws of the land, by concern and care for those who need help, by lifting up and exalting the Lord Jesus Christ at every opportunity, and by a constant outreach to those who not now know Jesus as their Lord and Savior. We can pray for Christian missionaries in all parts of the world, that God will protect them and use their witness mightily. We can pray for fellow Christians everywhere.

To become involved more and more as a citizen of the kingdom of God means that our prayer life will be more and more dedicated to the coming of that kingdom over all God's creation. As we seek what God's Word tells us is His will in all facets of life, we can be sure that our prayers will be in line with the will of God, and thus be assured of His open ears as we worship and adore Him, and together with the Holy Spirit seek for His will to be done on earth, beginning in our own lives.

About the Author

Author MILUM O. OWENS, Jr. has been serving in the Southern Baptist ministry for seventy years. He is a South Carolina native and graduated from Furman University, the Southern Baptist Theological Seminary, ThM; and Luther Rice Seminary, DMin.

Pastor Owens led in starting six Southern Baptist churches and has been interim pastor of sixteen others. He served one year as an interim Southern Baptist missionary in Belgium and also served in many capacities in the North Carolina Baptist State Convention. For many years, he was trustee at Gardner-Webb College (University). He was an early leader in the conservative effort, helping to bring the Southern Baptist Convention back to the Bible as the inspired, infallible, and authoritative Word of God.

He is the author of *Encouraging the Saints*, a commentary on II Corinthians, co-author of *The Word Made Flesh*, a commentary on the Gospel of John, and is publisher and editor of a small bi-monthly publication, *The Watchman*.

Printed in the United States
125081LV00006BB/1-168/P